DISAPPEARED

THE SEARCH FOR
JEAN MCCONVILLE

DISAPPEARED

THE SEARCH FOR JEAN McCONVILLE

BY SÉAMUS McKENDRY

BLACKWATER PRESS

Editor
Margaret Burns

Design/Layout
Paula Byrne

Cover
Liz Murphy

Maps
Denis Baker

ISBN
1 84131 473 0

© Séamus McKendry 2000

Produced in Ireland by
Blackwater Press
c/o Folens Publishers
Hibernian Industrial Estate,
Greenhills Road,
Tallaght, Dublin 24.

The author and Publisher would like to thank the following for photographs provided: Alan Lewis at Photo Press, Kelvin Boyes, Brendan Murphy and Pacemaker Press.

ACKNOWLEDGEMENTS

The fact that I wrote this account of events is due to Helen, my wife, who badgered me over many years into taking up the pen. In fact, I am glad she succeeded, for I consider myself honoured to tell the story of a woman, whom I regret I never met. A very special thank you is kept for John O'Connor of Blackwater Press for believing in me, when I didn't. I would like to thank John Manley and later Michael Mann, for tramping the streets with us, when it wasn't 'cool' to do so and the many politicians and figureheads who risked a lot by giving us support and advice. Of course, I must mention our children, who absolutely refused to take a back seat and I know never will. A very special thanks is reserved for those within the Republican Movement, especially 'the queer fella', who risked their lives so that we might begin living ours. I cannot finish without mentioning 'Joe Bloggs', or whatever it is you call that ordinary decent individual who, over those long arduous years of battling uphill, quite simply made us believe that it would be worth it. And it is!

CONTENTS

This short chronicle of brutality is dedicated to Jean McConville, her daughter Helen and our children, Jean's grandchildren, Sé, Kellyanne, Conor, Seán and Sinéad. Not forgetting Tiegan, Jean's great-grandaughter.

A PROMISE

I found myself learning the basics of carpentry, not because I felt it was my calling, but rather as a price for acting the 'hard man'. Most adolescents were not impressed by the daily gunbattles and riots of the 1970s; certain wannabes like myself were. While my contemporaries were sitting exams and devising methods of ridding themselves of virginity and acne, I was receiving schooling of the street kind, namely weapons instruction and survival techniques. Carpentry was my parents' idea.

Certainly I can, if pressured, produce the school reports which verify that I had the same yearning for academia as others, but the reality of my life meant that my interests lay elsewhere for the time being.

These early days proved a major shock for a young country boy who had just moved to Andersonstown from the relative backwoods of rural Co. Down. Conflict, up until now, had been the result of my father coming home on a Friday night after he had paid a visit to the pub, the bookies or more usually both. I doubt very much if the words Protestant, Unionist or Loyalist had entered my parent's vocabulary, never mind my own, yet they were soon to become the backbone of conversations which would last for the next thirty years. Surely my parents should have noticed the steady stream of traffic heading out of West Belfast when we first entered Andersonstown that cold March morning in 1968.

I guess in my formative years it was somewhat cool to be oppressed. To read about Che Guevara, Mao Tse Tung and other revolutionaries of their ilk, gave me a sense of camaraderie with those who had left their indelible mark on history. To man barricades at twelve or thirteen was not a bad life when you considered the hardship that was being inflicted on others, namely the thousands who had already lost their homes, (and quite often their lives) in the less secure areas of Belfast. Almost overnight, rioting became the national sport, certain individuals would be lauded for their feats of daring, just as others would be castigated for cowardice. Little did I know that the would-be academics would later be considered the lucky ones in all this turmoil.

House raids, or more correctly, house wreckings by the British Army were the order of the day. Initially the British Army had been welcomed by the majority of the Nationalist population, but the honeymoon period of tolerance was fast disappearing and youths queued to enlist in the IRA, both Official and Provisional. The Provisionals were formed in 1969 when a group from the Official IRA disagreed with the direction the Movement was taking. The Officials (or Stickies) ceased military operations in 1972 and the more hard-line Provisonals (or Provos) continued without rival.

School, which I was seeing less and less of every day, was no sanctuary from the war. It was quite common to be told to vacate a particular classroom as it offered a suitable sniping point to attack a nearby Army patrol. This was certainly not an environment that could be described as conducive to even the most basic of education.

Before long, the majority of youngsters my age were receiving 'street' education. This was when I began to learn about weapons and survival rather than calculus and literature. In an effort to keep me from the clutches of the paramilitaries, I was soon despatched to the Convent of the Sisters of Nazareth, where it was believed an apprenticeship in carpentry would quell the revolutionary spirit I possessed. The downside to this bastion of all that was Catholic and proper, was its location in the heart of Loyalist South East Belfast. It did, however, provide both sanctuary from the madness outside and, perhaps more importantly, the company of a hundred or so young girls, even if these unwilling charges were forever chaperoned by nuns and careworkers.

I concluded that before the revolution could really take off, I would have to be content with the mundane task of earning a living sawing pieces of wood for my Uncle, who was the maintenance contractor in the building. Although people were being slaughtered daily in the streets around me, I felt secure in the knowledge that I was learning a trade, being paid and was temporarily safe from the physcopaths who were killing for God, for Ulster and for God knows what else. Some considered me lucky to be surrounded by dozens of teenage girls, but to be honest, the journey to and from work was fraught with danger. The sense of security would evaporate as soon as I left through the gates at night, almost immediately a fear would grip; every individual, every car was potentially the bringer of death. I became haunted, obsessed even, by the masked unknowns who toured the construction sites looking for Catholic victims. I would regularly visualise the gang of killers who had just recently singled out my seventeen-year-old friend Robbie as he played a lunchtime game of chess with his workmate. Forced to kneel, he had had his youth and intellect blown around the room. I often thought that life on the dole would be better than this constant stress, my father however, disagreed. His constant lectures ensured I would remain in employment, whatever the risks. A better reason for my daily brush with death, was the chance of getting to know the tall, good-looking, skinny lass whom I had been scrutinising at the convent for some time now. I did everything in my power to make in-roads but she just didn't want to know. I had to resign myself to figuring that it was her loss, as there can't have been many urban guerrillas (with carpentry skills) working in the Convent.

After a particularly harrowing incident, when I was pursued by a mob of Loyalists and came within inches of joining Robbie, I concluded enough was enough. The tall skinny girl, whose mother had deserted her ten children, would have to make do with some lesser mortal; I was determined to live a while longer. With the North determined to commit suicide, life took on a hectic pace and the daily riots and gunbattles were surpassed only by the carnage unleashed in Belfast where the Provos experimented with home-made explosives and Loyalists chopped up Catholics for the fun of it. House raids and beatings at the hands of the RUC and British Army did little to dissuade me from retaliation, and being arrested and detained in Police or Army Barracks became a way of life.

As more and more friends appeared in the obituary columns, I wondered if there was another more humane way of fighting for the cause. Hoping to steer clear of the more militant factions, I joined the Official's political wing, Republican Clubs. A steady diet of Marx and James Connolly was teaching me to respect the socialist method of securing my aspirations. Politics was to become the way of the urban guerrilla; even though I still believed certain deaths were acceptable.

It was soon Spring 1975 and Her Majesty's Government realised they had made an error in judgement, or rather hadn't enough evidence to secure a conviction, for I was released from Long Kesh (or the Maze) prison where I had been incarcerated for the lengthy period of two months. Okay, it was only a couple of months, but this was enough to make me a felon, and my social status soared accordingly.

I was not slow to notice that girls would go out of their way to be seen with this hardened revolutionary. A celebratory evening in a Twinbrook social club provided an unexpected surprise, I was once again to meet Helen, the tall, skinny focus of my attentions who had shunned me the previous year. She was working as a waitress, looking better than ever and, for the extra bonus, was unattached and undoubtedly bowled over by my newly-acquired demeanour — we strode home arm in arm. The big romance blossomed and within months we were talking of marriage.

Needless to say, my parents and others were absolutely appalled at the thought of teenagers being wed, but even more appalling was the fact that I was considering marrying a girl from a broken home; someone whose mother had 'gone off with a battalion commander of the Ulster Defence Association'. When I recounted this tale to Helen, I could immediately sense her hurt. Although she had heard all the stories before, this one and much worse, they never ceased to strike at the heart of her. I guess it was easier for me to believe the rumours than to accept Helen's suggestion that her mother might have been taken by the IRA and murdered. The IRA was, after all, the protector of the Nationalist people.

Anyway, I was intent on marrying Helen and not her background. We decided to leave the past behind us and plans were made that would enable us to begin a new life away from the conflict. Liverpool, England was chosen as Helen had some relatives there. Our elopement was short-lived though, because as soon as we set foot on English soil, I was arrested under The Prevention of Terrorism Act and the Bridewell Prison became home for the next few days. Here I was interrogated night and day by an inept Special Branch which had out-of-date information and little knowledge of the conflict, but Helen was to fare even worse. This very courteous Police Force, after promising to take her to her relations' house had, in fact, dropped her twelve miles in the opposite direction. Quite alone in a strange and anti-Irish environment, I considered her very fortunate to be able to tell me of her harrowing ordeal. Unable to escape the hassle in the North, and obviously not welcome in Britain, we made do with what we had and were married in Andersonstown, near my parent's home, on 6 March 1976 at the tender age of eighteen years.

Something I hadn't bargained on was a ready-made family. Soon I was father to Helen's younger siblings: Michael (Mickey), Thomas (Tucker), Suzanne, Billy and Jim. We were to be their foster parents at holiday periods. Michael, who absolutely refused to return to his orphanage, moved in on a permanent basis. On my meagre wages as an apprentice carpenter and with no financial help from Social Services, things began to disintegrate and quarrels were commonplace.

Amidst the turmoil of these early years, I foolishly promised Helen that I would seek out the truth regarding her mother. At the time, I wasn't to know that this simple promise would lead us both on a journey which would last for the best part of thirty years and change our lives and the lives of others like us in the North. Undoubtedly, hidden forces would make sure our quest for the truth would be a prolonged and difficult one.

I soon learned the hard way that to ask questions in war torn 1970s Belfast was unwise and not a little dangerous. A method I used in the early days was to enter known Provisional haunts and bring the conversation round to pigeons (Helen's father and brothers had raced pigeons for years). After a while I would drop in the name McConville: 'Whatever happened to those people? Do they still live in Belfast, and wasn't there some sort of story about the mother being a tout?'

Invariably, no matter how clever I thought I was, I would be told to 'Fuck off!' On one occasion I was dramatically cut short when I was shown the butt of a revolver. This pathetic little game of trying to glean some tit-bit of information was to be played out for the next twenty-plus years.

Even though Helen was adamant that her mother had been abducted by the Provisionals, we didn't stop looking elsewhere. Letters were despatched to the Salvation Army, the Social Services and just anybody anywhere who might have come across Jean McConville. One of Helen's greatest fears was of her mother surviving the abduction, but not the ensuing trauma. We hoped she had been forced into exile, lost her memory and was now living in some mental institution, her identity a secret, even to herself. This theory was reinforced by a postcard the family had received in 1973 with a Blackpool, England postmark.

Although unsigned it offered a glimmer of hope.

What little information I begrudgingly received from Republicans also echoed the England theory. Firstly, Jean was not from a Republican family or background and it was therefore highly unlikely she would be privy to anything that might endanger their members or operations. Secondly, she was a mother of ten young children and I was assured that 'although Loyalists would think nothing of killing a young widowed mother, Republicans had a strict code of conduct and women and children were exempt from the harsher methods of inner policing'. Sure enough up until now, the traditional method of punishing females who had supposedly transgressed was the centuries-old 'Tar and Feather', or in extreme cases the individual would be shipped off to England to face a life away from family and friends.

Two stories appeared with most regularity; the first claimed that she had absconded with not one, but several members of the British Army and the other that she had been living with a known Loyalist commander in East Belfast. 'Impeccable' sources would describe at length how she had started her second family with this paramilitary. This was nothing short of miraculous as Jean had had a hysterectomy back in 1966.

A BELFAST GIRL

Helen was fifteen when her mother disappeared. She had seen Jean as a friend and soulmate and not just her mum, it was therefore doubly hurtful to be told that her mother had not just betrayed the cause, but Helen too.

Born the second of five children to Thomas and May Murray at 113 Avoniel Road, Belfast, there was nothing to indicate that someday this unamazing little girl would become a household name. Her father was a stereotypical East Belfast Protestant who provided for his family secure in the knowledge that he would have a lifetime's employment in the Harland & Wolff shipyard. Their two-up, two-down terraced home was just around the corner from the world famous yard. Jean's childhood skyline was totally dominated by the gigantic cranes. Morning and night thousands of men would tramp past her door as they clocked on or off shifts in the yard.

Schooling for girls was no priority in the fifties and so Jean was despatched as a young teen into domestic service. It was here on Holywood Road, employed by a family, that she met Arthur McConville, who soon wooed her with his tales of military action in the British Army. An only child and some twelve years her elder, he had, like his father and grandfather before him, run off to war at the age of seventeen. The naïve little Belfast girl was besotted by this young veteran who had fought the Japanese in Burma. With her now widowed mother May's guarded blessing, the pair were married in 1952. The fact that Arthur was Roman Catholic didn't matter to May, though she was often rebuked in her family circle for allowing a 'Fenian' across the door.

Helen remarks fondly that Arthur, at six-foot-four and physically very fit must have cut a strange figure against the diminutive Jean who was five-foot-two in her shoes. Jean's parents' house at Avoniel Road became home and they soon began their family of ten children: Anne, Robert, Arthur Jnr (Archie), Helen, Agnes, Micheal (Mickey), Thomas (Tucker), Suzanne and twins Billy and Jim. A burden that would plague the young family presented itself almost immediately when Anne, their first born, suffered terrible brain damage when she fell from her pram. For the rest of her days she would require special help.

Tours of duty began to take their toll and after many quarrels it was decided that Arthur would leave the Army, which he did in 1964. Upon receipt of his pension he set up a small building repair business.

In the belief that the children would be better served if both parents shared the same religion, Jean decided to change to Catholicism. This was something she took extremely seriously and she was a regular visitor to Clonard Monastery for Catholic instruction. It was really only when the first of their children started 'the wrong' kind of primary school that the young family endured any kind of aggression. In the Summer of 1966, a very frightened ten-year-old Archie was pulled from the middle of a bonfire where a gang of Loyalists had tried to use him as a Guy. The following February, with Jean ill in hospital (thrombosis was a recurring problem), Arthur and young Michael were savagely beaten by another mob of thugs and hospitalised. Although very little would be said in front of the children, they sensed worse was to come. The local Orange bands would make a point of starting their parade from the McConville's door. Helen recalls that everyone spoke in whispers and one particularly good friend would visit the home daily to recount the most recent evictions of Catholics. It was soon the turn of the McConvilles, a gun was placed at Arthur's head, and he was told to get out and take his Fenian bastards with him.

Arthur was slipped out by a friend in the middle of the night; he naïvely believed the family would be spared if he went. At first, 'light' Loyalists stoned the house and Arthur's friend received a gunshot to the leg for showing support. The next evening the family had a visit from the RUC and a Protestant clergyman who begged Jean to change religion so that they might be protected; she refused. Hearing that Arthur had safely reached his mother's home in the Catholic Springhill, West Belfast, they packed what they could and tried unsuccessfully to acquire a taxi. Incredibly, it was the RUC who finally managed to secure one, yet they were to stand idly by when the cab was attacked by a mob. The frightened taxi driver would take the family no further than the main Falls Road and the distraught refugees were forced to walk the rest of the way.

The sanctuary of Mary McConville's was short-lived as Jean and her mother-in-law had never seen eye to eye. In a very short while, Jean, Arthur and the children had packed up and moved to St Thomas's School on the Whiterock Road. Practically every school in West Belfast was housing refugees in 1969. Soon they would be shifted to yet another school, St Louise's, but living on the classroom floors was proving detrimental to Jean's health. The joy at being offered an emergency chalet in Beechmount was fleeting, as squatters got there first. The same dilemma was repeated with a chalet on the Shaws Road. Even though St Louise's was trying desperately to return to normal, Arthur refused to leave until guaranteed accommodation. New chalets were being erected in Divis Street and, when offered one of these, Arthur stayed with the workmen to prevent losing this home to the squatters. The family stayed here until being given a maisonette at No. 3 Farset Walk in the sprawling Divis Flats in February 1970.

The new home was far from ideal, but it did at least allow for eighteen-year-old Anne to stay with the family at weekends. With Arthur unemployed and the war raging all around them, it was becoming more and more of a struggle to visit the little girl so tragically injured as an infant. Anne was being cared for at Muckamore Abbey Hospital in Antrim. As there were no state benefits to help with the care of nursing a handicapped child, the family had to struggle hard to make ends meet. Four-year-old Billy became the next worry for the distraught couple when he was rushed to hospital with kidney trouble. In the end, he had a kidney removed.

About this time, Jean heard that her mother had been assaulted by Loyalist paramilitaries for refusing to contribute to their cause. Helen recalls that, despite the terrible trauma endured, they still managed to share a joke together and relished their twice-weekly excursion up the road to the Hibs (Ancient Order of Hibernians), or if the area was relatively quiet, to St Matthew's, for their only luxury in life, Bingo. In all the bedlam they were still capable of laughter. They had to have a strong sense of humour when they returned home one day to find the pigeon-loving Archie and Michael had sectioned off half their bedroom to accommodate the thirty or so birds they had just purchased!

Having survived the three-day Falls Road curfew, when the area was sealed off while the Army searched and arrested in the Summer of 1971, the family was to receive a further crashing blow. Arthur had been poorly for some time now, but refused to burden his doctor or family. Jean realised something serious was wrong when he was unable to hold a cup of tea. The ensuing hospital tests confirmed that Arthur had cancer of the lung. In October of 1971 he would have it removed.

His condition did not improve and the living room became his bedroom. Helen recalls trying to feed him the day before Christmas Eve, unaware that he had been in a coma for most of the day. He passed away on 3 January 1972 in the arms of his young son Archie and was buried in the family plot in Lisburn, leaving his distraught wife Jean to rear their ten children.

Try as she might, Jean was finding it impossible to shake off the heavy depression that enveloped her. Northern Ireland had just entered its bloodiest year ever and death and destruction prevailed. The oldest son, Robert, was next in line to suffer the family's bad luck. He had (like so many other young lads) fallen foul of the Security Forces. They promised he would be imprisoned on his seventeenth birthday and true to their word on 21 March, his birthday, he was arrested and interned on the prison ship, Maidstone.

Robert's arrest, Arthur's death, lack of money and the unrelenting bloodshed in the surrounding streets finally took their toll and Jean made her first attempt at suicide. After two more overdoses, it was accepted that this was no cry for help and she was sent to a psychiatric hospital. This was the first of many spells in a number of psychiatric hospitals.

By agreement with the Social Services, fourteen-year-old Helen was permitted to refrain from school to take care of the children. Jean, a shadow of her former self, was allowed to return to her family in the early Summer. She became something of a recluse, venturing out only to visit Robert in prison or purchase a few groceries. In these days, it was commonplace to be harassed by the security forces, both in the home and on the street. Helen and her friend Eileen were singled out by one particular Regiment for threats and abuse which resulted in Eileen being shot in the face with a baton round. The pair was rushed south to Dundalk, where the Red

Cross arranged digs and employment, until the offending Regiment finished their tour of duty.

Helen returned a month later to the mayhem that was 1972 Belfast, gunbattles were a daily occurrence. It was during a particularly long battle that the family became aware of someone or something thumping against the front of the house. Moments later, crying could be heard, this gradually got louder: 'Somebody help me, please God I don't want to die, help me please.' Without hesitation, Jean rose from the floor where the family had lain so many times during shooting. The children were ordered to stay put, but through the now open door they watched their mother whisper a prayer as she cradled a young British soldier's head. His colleagues soon arrived and spirited him away. When she came back in she seemed very upset as she washed the blood from her hands. Prophetically, sixteen-year-old Archie warned that it wasn't the cleverest thing to do whereupon he received a swift crack on the ear for his input as Jean reminded him that even British soldiers were somebody's children. By morning, a slogan reading 'Brit Lover' had been written on the door and the remainder of the paint thrown about the front of the house. The following evening windows were broken as the locals expressed their displeasure at Jean's humanity.

Most sickening of all, the children's pet labradors, Provo and Stickie (ironically called after the two IRA factions) were thrown into the rubbish chute, where they perished.

Although Jean was missing her mother terribly, she made do with writing, as travelling to East Belfast would probably have been worse than the present abuse. Jean's defiance is well illustrated by her refusal to stop going to Bingo even though she had been warned she was lucky (being an Orange bastard) to reside in the area at all.

Gradually the hassle diminished, only to restart over the purchase of a second-hand suite some weeks later. Bought in good faith from a strong Republican family, trouble erupted when Jean was asked for more than the agreed price. Refusing to pay any more, she asked the family to take the furniture back and reimburse her. They refused and the aggravation continued for weeks, snide remarks and scurrilous rumour were the order of the day. At this time, the favoured method of moving weapons if a house was being raided by the Army was to pass them via the outside windows to your neighbour, who would do likewise until the arms would eventually be far removed from the soldiers. Jean had earlier that year refused to participate in 'the chain' for fear of having another child imprisoned and was now being constantly rebuked about it.

A very strange incident was to follow: upon answering a knock at the door, Helen was set upon and beaten by a gang of local girls. Incredibly, when confronted by an angry Jean, the girls claimed they had been paid to carry out the attack by Mary, Helen's paternal grandmother. Mary now lived nearby and was friendly with the Republican family who had been causing Jean and her family so much grief recently. Whether there was any truth in their story or not, it was safe to say that the animosity between Jean and her mother-in-law had not abated.

Jean had continually suspected that the gas heating in their home at No. 3 Farset Walk was responsible for aggravating young Michael's asthma. She had requested an exchange to somewhere with a different heating system and was very surprised when handed the keys of No. 2 St Jude's Walk. All day on 6 December 1972, the family packed their belongings in preparation for the next day's 200 metre flit. This was Tuesday, Bingo night, but Jean had decided already that there was too much to do and anyway, Christmas was just three short weeks away and money for leisure was in short supply. That evening her chum Bernie arrived as usual, offering to pay for the 'treat' and soon the pair were making towards the Cullingtree Road Youth and Social Club.

Helen answered the door a while later to a distraught Bernie who asked Helen if she was alright. 'Why wouldn't I be?', replied Helen 'and where's my mummy?' Bernie told how the doorman had whispered in Jean's ear that one of the children had been injured, and a lift was outside to take her to the children's hospital. Bernie offered to accompany her but it was suggested she stay on and finish marking the books.

Bewildered, Helen and Bernie remained for half an hour in the house before heading up the Falls to the Royal Hospital. The staff declared that they had not treated nor heard from anyone by the name of McConville that evening. Thoughts raced around in Helen's head as she made her way back to the flat, she expected to see her mum as she walked in the door, but this was not the case. The time dragged in until about 2.30 a.m. when there was loud thumping at the door.

The officer in charge of the Army patrol believed they had a Mrs McConville in the barracks, whom they had found wandering in a very distressed condition in McDonald Street, off the Grosvenor Road. He suggested that Helen bring a coat and shoes and offered her a lift, which was declined. As Helen approached the Albert Street Barracks she was aware of hysterical screaming; her mother's screaming. Racing in she found a bedraggled, shoeless figure. On seeing Helen, Jean managed a semblance of composure, she hurriedly drank a cup of tea and donned the coat and slippers Helen had brought. Only sobbing could be heard as they made the short journey back home. Bernie reluctantly said goodnight and Jean shook uncontrollably as she related the night's brutal sequence of events.

A young woman waiting at the Bingo hall door claimed Helen had been struck by a car, Jean had been told not to panic as a car waited to take her to the Hospital. She was then pushed onto the floor of the motor and a hood was placed on her head. Although unable to see, she ascertained that the building she was eventually taken to was derelict. While tied to a chair she was questioned, screamed at and violently beaten about the head and body. The 'interrogation' continued with more and more intensity until, unexpectantly, her tormentors fell silent. Realising she had been alone for some time now, Jean managed to free herself and ran for her life. Her next recollection was of delight at seeing Helen and Bernie.

When Helen asked her mother, 'What questions?', Jean replied: 'A load of nonsense, stuff I knew nothing about.' She would only say it had been the IRA and that it must have been a mistake since she knew nothing about their goings-on and nor did she want to. Helen implored her to slip off to granny's in East Belfast, but Jean said that they were, 'not going to lose another home', and reiterated her bewilderment at the beating and interrogation. She wasn't guilty of anything and was not running from anyone.

The belief that things would blow over dwindled when Helen watched as her Mum struggled to carry furniture towards the door for a makeshift barricade. Neither Jean nor her anxious daughter would sleep that night, and Helen watched as her still shaking mother removed tuft after tuft of loose clumps of hair.

In the morning, the younger children were despatched to school as normal, unaware of the brutality that had occurred the previous night. Helen stayed at home to help with the move to St Jude's Walk, but couldn't help but notice how her mother silently struggled against pain to carry out the tasks at hand. By now, the eye that was reddened last night was turning black and the dried areas of lip indicated where cuts had been inflicted. Later, the children would arrive back from school and Helen listened to conversation for the first time that day. Jean had spent practically the whole day in silence, no doubt trying to make sense of what had happened.

The electric cooker had yet to be connected, so Jean instructed Helen to go and purchase fish and chips for the supper. 'Hurry up, and don't be stopping for a sneaky smoke', Jean added before retiring to the scalding hot bath which she hoped would give some relief to her aching body. Some twenty minutes later, as she made her way through the labyrinth that was Divis, it struck Helen as odd that so many people should be standing out on the balconies. This was commonplace in the Summer months, but certainly not in mid-December. Nearing home, people were staring and whispering. Correctly fearing the worst, Helen began to run at breakneck speed towards the screaming children's voices. On entering the flat she was almost knocked down as her hysterical siblings attempted to recount the horror of the last ten minutes. Archie was ashen-faced and shaking as he blurted out what had happened.

The IRA had burst in, eight men and four women in total, and ordered the terrified youngsters upstairs at gun-point and dragged the screeching, pleading young mother from her bath, claiming they only wanted to talk to her for half an hour. The youngsters, who had by now rushed back down again, were beaten back by heartless thugs who proceeded to drag the poor woman through the Flats complex after allowing her to quickly get dressed. Archie, who defiantly stayed with them until a gun was put to his head, stood helpless as his mother was shoved into the back of a waiting Volkswagen camper van. On being told to 'Fuck off or be shot', the tear-strewn sixteen-year-old ran home.

For hours they sat waiting for Jean's return. Eventually, Helen prepared the young ones for bed, promising them that if they stopped crying, 'mummy would be home when they woke'. The moment the children were asleep, Helen and Archie went out to search the area. Beginning in McDonald Street, where Jean had been found the previous night, they looked in every old building they came across. Having trodden the streets for hours, they returned home to ponder what had happened.

Archie assured Helen that nothing terrible would happen, that even if the IRA had mistaken their mother for someone who had done something serious, the punishment would be no worse than tarring and feathering or a shaven head.

On Archie's suggestion, the confused and terrified young pair left the next morning for *The Nail-bomb*, a shebeen that was a known Provo haunt on Cullingtree Road. They asked to speak to someone about their mother and were given Coke and crisps while they waited. The senior IRA person who listened to their impassioned plea for information, said in a low voice that not all Republicans 'had hearts of stone', although he didn't help and wasn't heard from again.

By now, thirteen-year-old Agnes had gone to live with Granny Mary and Archie would do likewise following a row with Helen about his friends not treating the home with respect. That evening, Helen took the twins, aged only six, to Mary's, hoping a bite of supper could be provided. She found the grandmother in the company of some cronies, drinking and partaking of fish and chips. When asked if there might be a bite for the wee-ones, Helen was pinned to the wall by one of the granny's companions who told her to 'fuck off, and go begging for food on the Loyalist Shankill Road, where her whore of a mother plied her trade'.

Thankfully, later that night, Mary and Colette, two of Helen's pals, seized the chance to smuggle a few odds and ends from their own kitchens. They also helped carry all the furniture from downstairs to the upstairs bedrooms, where Helen felt it might be safer.

The following three weeks were an abyss of hunger, fear, exhaustion and utter confusion. Total apathy had by now enveloped Helen, she could see no way out of this unbearable predicament and had confided to her few friends that if it wasn't for the little ones she would honestly 'do herself in'. Meanwhile, her pals had concocted a scheme for providing the little ones with presents for Christmas, they suggested going into the city centre on a thieving spree. Nancy Tomelty, a well-respected member of the Divis community, unintentionally put a stop to the shopping expedition when she arrived on the doorstep to enquire about the family's welfare. Helen was ordered to fetch her coat and was marched to the local store, where, after filling a trolley with groceries, the shop owner left Helen speechless when he produced a number of toys which he claimed Jean had paid for in full. Tears filled her eyes as she made her way back home, for she knew Nancy and the storekeeper had concocted the story quite simply to disguise their humanity; something that was undoubtedly lacking in the area. Within hours, an electrician arrived to connect the cooker and the family could now have something warm to eat.

Shortly after that miserable Christmas, where toys remained unplayed with, the RUC arrived to say Michael and Thomas, now aged eleven and eight, had been arrested. They wanted one of the parents to come and fetch them. Helen informed them that her father was dead and her mother had not been seen or heard of for weeks. Incredibly, they never bothered to ask any more and Helen was allowed to collect the children herself without any trouble.

On 3 January 1973, an incident occurred that should have indicated to Helen that her mother was not coming back. A rather nervous young man (remotely familiar), called at the home and asked for Helen by name. He proceeded to hand over a purse that was instantly recognisable as Jean's. Helen begged for some knowledge of her mum's whereabouts, but the man said he knew nothing and was only doing as he had been instructed.

On inspection, the purse appeared to contain the amount of money expected, but also, chillingly, three rings: wedding, engagement and eternity — her mother's rings. What could this cryptic message mean? Helen exhausted herself trying to figure out the significance of it all, and although she prepared herself to go to the Police, she knew she never would. To do so would endanger her mother even more, as people were regularly killed for less.

The callousness of the 'neighbours' was difficult enough to comprehend, but why did the priests of the parish ignore them? Why weren't they inundated by social workers or truancy officers? No one had been seen at school for over a month; did the teachers fail to notice that half the cast for the Nativity play was missing? Did the Police who were regular visitors to the flat (to complain about something or other), never think to demand the whereabouts of the children's mother?

Archie and his pals did little to ease the burden when they used the place as a hang-out for their cronies. At her wits' end, on 15 January, Helen grabbed a coat and headed for the Northern Ireland Civil Rights Association's office in Belfast's King Street. She poured out her incredible story to a totally astonished member of staff, who hurriedly asked for tea and a sandwich to be brought in. Helen could not figure out whether it was the compassion being shown by this gentleman or the ham and cheese sandwich, which she devoured greedily and with a sense of guilt, that pleased her most. After promising to do all in his power to assist, he produced a ten-pound note from his own pocket, instructing Helen to give the children a good feed and, with the remainder, treat herself to a box of chocolates for her courage.

True to his word, an article highlighting the plight of the McConville family appeared in the organisation's magazine that very week. Soon everyone wanted to know about the forgotten family. Media teams fought for the best angles, and the previously unseen newspaper reporters arrived in swarms to glean something from the confused youngsters.

The media circus did not abate until the RUC arrived and dispersed them. These were policemen and policewomen that the children had never encountered before; they did not carry guns or hostility and were instead full of diplomacy and understanding. Unbelievably though, the Police, and the welfare workers that accompanied them, left the family on their own for another week. This was in spite of the fact that, as Helen overheard, the younger ones had told the Police the names of some of Jean's abductors as quite a few of them lived in the neighbourhood; one woman was even brash enough to be unmasked at the time.

Michael Glass, a case officer for Social Services, was soon to arrive to inform Helen that they would have to be taken into the care of the State. Helen pleaded for leniency as their mother would be home any day now, and anyway she would do her best to improve things, making sure the wee-ones would be at school etc. Glass was unrelenting, claiming they had received too many complaints from neighbours in recent days. The same 'neighbours' who had turned their backs and ignored the family for so long, suddenly appeared caring and compassionate. The marauding Press packs might have been fooled, but the McConville family would neither forgive nor forget.

Sack upon sack of mail had begun to arrive. There were letters from ordinary folk the length and breadth of the British Isles; some contained prayers (that just couldn't be eaten) others would have anything from £5–£20 notes. Helen recalls vividly a letter from an eighty-six-year-old in Drogheda, lauding her with praise and how she cried when she discovered a £10 note in the bottom of the envelope.

News of the change in fortune travelled fast and before long Granny Mary was on hand to supervise the mail and the Press. Reporters arrived, as agreed, to interview Helen, but she was pushed aside by Mary and Archie, who went on to say that there was no crisis. They admitted the IRA had taken Jean, but they were assured she would not be harmed and indeed would be returned shortly. Soon MPs Gerry Fitt and Paddy Devlin would come on board. They visited the granny's flat where the children were now welcomed with open arms. Promising to do all in their power to resolve the predicament, they left after tea and biscuits with granny. The politicians released a statement to the Press the next day.

> We want to find out where Mrs McConville is but we cannot do so because of the amount of publicity that the case is being given. She is afraid that reporters will find out where she is and therefore she will not come out of hiding. We do not believe that she is being held captive. The publicity was necessary in the first instance. It has brought about an expression of horror that this woman should have been treated in this way and it has turned opinion against the people responsible for driving her away. But the publicity should be eased off if it is preventing her from returning. We are appealing to the people involved to say that no more violence will be used against this woman. I don't think there is anything else that can be done.
>
> *Irish News 19 January 1973*

When, in 1996, I asked Mr Devlin how he could have been so sure Jean was not being held captive, he claimed that Gerry Fitt had been assured by leading Republicans of this fact. Sadly, the media interest waned as the MPs had hoped and sure enough Helen and the younger children found themselves back in the flat with a connected cooker but nothing to cook and lights that they were too frightened to use. They had served their purpose at granny's.

This was to be the last straw for Helen. When Mr Glass called the next day, she practically pleaded with him to take her and the others into care, so that they might at least be fed and bathed. A crack in their tub prevented it being even halfway filled. Glass's job had now been made easier for him and within a short while two cars arrived to ferry Helen, Michael, Thomas, Suzanne and twins Jim and Billy off to the

Nazareth Lodge Children's Home on the Ravenhill Road. Helen remembers telling the kids it would only be for a little while, 'till Mummy comes back from England'. There were no goodbyes or farewell kisses from the 'neighbours' who perched nosily on their balconies.

'Fuck yous all', Helen whispered as she entered the car.

THE LODGE

Uncertainty flooded Helen's head as they drove across the city. Should she have somehow fought a bit harder to maintain the home? Surely she could have taken a job somewhere. She took comfort though from the kindly Michael Glass, who promised that they would be kept together until their mother decided it was safe enough to return for them. Anyway, hadn't Paddy Devlin assured them that in a few short weeks a foster home and family would be waiting for them in the newly-constructed Twinbrook Estate? The young ones cried as they drove through the gates of Nazareth Lodge. The towering five-storey red brick building appeared like something from *The Addam's Family* television series and this eerie vista frightened them even more.

Taken to what was known as the Nursery, the family huddled together on a large settee for what appeared hours. Too scared to move, they whispered as they guessed what might be in store for them. Finally Glass returned to bid them goodbye, said he would return at the weekend, and introduced the good-natured young nun, Sister Monica. The house rules were listed in a gentle southern accent and the family relaxed a little. The six-year-olds, Jim and Billy began to babble on about their mummy coming for them soon. These innocent ramblings were curtailed when the young nun pointed out, quite forcefully, that here there were no Murphy, Muldoon or McConville families, from here on they would be part of 'The Lodge' and that family only. Talk of past lives was strictly forbidden, as was inquiring into the background of others.

Supper was greedily and gratefully taken, but on seeing the dormitory, the young ones became hysterical and begged Helen to take them home. To pacify them, Helen was allowed a curtained-off bed in the corner of the huge room. Morning bewildered them even more when the nuns checked the beds; a dry one was rewarded with a chocolate bar whilst a wet one earned the poor perpetrator 'a smack on the arse'. Accepting someone other than their mother to chastise them caused many problems initially. Eventually, the children were togged out for school, which was housed in the building. Helen, having missed so much education in the past couple of years, became very self-conscious and point-blank refused to attend. Amazingly, she was not forced to go and instead spent her days helping with domestic chores around the Home.

Thinking that Jean might by now have returned, Helen implored the Mother Superior to allow her to go home at the weekend but, not surprisingly, she was refused. Determined, however, she pretended to run an errand and took a bus to the city centre and walked to the old home in Divis. On entering the flat she was astonished to find not her mother, but instead a drunk who had made himself quite at home. Personal items and anything of any value had been looted. Had a family, her family, ever lived here?

Seeing how distraught Helen was, an old friend sneaked her into her bedroom for the night. Glass was to find her the next day as she walked the streets in search of her mother. Whilst walking around, Helen had noticed a family being moved from a house that would soon be demolished. She told young Michael about it and the very next weekend, the pair had run away to implement the plan that had occupied Helen's mind all week long.

They returned to the flat and carried their bunk beds through the streets to the condemned house on Cullingtree

Road, forced open the nailed-up door, erected the beds, brushed up a little and made their way back to the orphanage.

Helen apologised to the Sisters of Nazareth for absconding and, having adhered to the rules for the following week, was granted permission to take the whole family to the park on the Saturday morning. That afternoon, they were a family again with a roof over their heads, a fireplace of sorts and beds to sleep in. Although they had food and shelter at the orphanage, their real hunger was for some news of their mother's whereabouts; as long as they were stuck in the orphanage, they weren't out looking for her. For the next two weeks they trudged streets and alleyways in the forlorn hope of spotting Jean, who they knew must be at her wits' end with worry about them. The attempt at independence didn't last long and when welfare officers swooped on the house after just two weeks, they were taken back to 'the Lodge'. Angry with Helen for breaking the rules and their trust, the nuns transferred her to a single room adjacent to their quarters. Billy, the baby of the family, pined constantly for his mother and was no stranger to sneaking round to Helen's room in the middle of the night for comfort. Early one morning, she woke to find an angry nun thrashing and screaming at Billy, Helen received a slap on the face when she protested that he was missing his mum. 'And anyway', she asked, 'where was the harm in her six-year-old brother sharing her bed?' She recalls being referred to as a bastard and a number, which stripped her of her identity, and she swore there and then to leave for good.

A uniform was fetched and she found herself attending school for the first time in some two years. It was an impossible situation as she had fallen so far behind in her studies. After another couple of weeks herself and Mickey were off again. A chance encounter with Archie in the city centre led them to Twinbrook, where Granny Mary now resided. Archie had promised there would be no problem staying there. Indeed, Archie was welcomed with open arms, but Helen was told in no uncertain terms she could stay the night only. Walking the streets of Divis the next day, she encountered Colette, an old pal who took her home to see her mother. This lady was not afraid to befriend a McConville and contacted the Social Services, who agreed Helen could stay in the short term. A semblance of normality came to Helen's life and she found herself joining the local youth club.

On a journey into town, a surprise lay in store; she met up with big brother Robert who had just been released from prison. They went to the Great Victoria Street Bus Station, where the curse of the McConvilles reared its ugly head once again. The station had been bombed just a few weeks previously and as Helen stood talking, one of the huge roofing trusses decided to give way, crashing onto her foot, removing half her big toe in the process. Hospitalised for ten days she was very fortunate to be allowed to go off for six weeks with the youth club to The Netherlands for the first true holiday of her life.

On her return, she made straight for Twinbrook, for Robert had told her she could stay regardless of the granny. Squatting was rife in the seventies and big brother soon had a flat for himself, Archie, Agnes and Helen. It soon turned sour, however, when Robert, just a teenager himself, found it impossible to balance what little money there was. They discovered they were eating less now than when they had been left on their own just after Jean's disappearance. One or two neighbours rallied to help, but in a very short while the Welfare were involved again.

Towards the end of 1973, the young family were on the move yet again, this time the Social Services took them to stay with the Smith family on the Palmerston Road. Things were great to begin with, as they had a kind, gentle couple to care for them and Granny Murray could be visited, as she lived close by. These short visits to the Avoniel Road provided

Helen with the only opportunity to talk to an adult about her mother. The Police, the Media and even the Social Services had given up on Jean McConville a long time ago, it was as if she had been a figment of the children's imagination. The brief respite ended when other children arrived to stay with the Smiths and one by one the kids were farmed out to orphanages, near and far. The promise to keep them together was sounding very hollow indeed.

Michael, the habitual runaway, was sent to the more secure 'Kircubbin', a Christian Brothers Boys Home, while Thomas, Suzanne and twins Billy and Jim would be returned to 'the Lodge'. Helen and her sister Agnes, who had now joined the band of nomads, were despatched to the Good Shepherd Convent on the Ormeau Road.

At weekends, Helen would be allowed to go 'home' to stay with friends. One evening, as she prepared to go to a film show in the parish hall, Helen was subjected to abuse about her mother having run off with a 'Brit'. A desperate course of action followed where she raided her pal's medicine cupboard and attempted to end her anguish. She would come round three days later, to discover the family who had given her shelter, hadn't even called a doctor but instead the Social Services. She realised that nobody gave a damn, yet she managed to hold herself together until Easter 1974 when she was officially (at age sixteen) allowed to leave the system of 'care' which she loathed so much. Almost unbelievably, Helen was presented with a pound note, and told: 'You're a big girl and old enough to make your own way in life.'

Returning to Twinbrook, where friends had promised to give her shelter, she was soon employed with a stitching company who manufactured shrouds for the recently departed while waitressing in the evenings and weekends.

A CLOSED BOOK

It was around this time that I once again encountered Helen and I believe I was attracted as much by her secretiveness as I was by her looks. The wedding present offered by a friend, a house and employment for the rest of my days in Western Australia, was regrettably declined when Helen point-blank refused to abandon the hope of tracing her mother. Anyway, we now had a part-time family in her siblings and couldn't take them all with us.

These were days of asking questions but receiving little or nothing in the form of answers. Around this time, I began to build a trusting relationship with a pretty senior member of the Provisionals, always known to myself as 'the queer fella'. We had been close pals since we were children, although our politics differed hugely. The same boyo thought nothing of planting a bomb in a crowded thoroughfare. His attitude would be that if there were civilians killed, then that was tough; to him the ends justified the means. I could not agree of course, and debates were often quite vocal. Although our opinions differed greatly, I thoroughly relished meeting him to discuss the progress of his war. Regarding the whereabouts of Jean, he would only reply that it was a 'closed book' and not for discussion. For years to come I would torture him on this subject, in the vain hope that he might someday ask the questions that I couldn't. His warnings, that I was going the right way about getting my head perforated, went unheeded.

When Helen knew I had spoken to someone in the Republican Movement her spirits would lift. When she thought

31

I was doing nothing, she became deeply upset and would lapse into serious bouts of depression. I could never really understand why she was so obsessed with discovering the truth. I realised that her mother had been cruelly taken away from her and most probably murdered, but why did the rest of her family not suffer to the same degree? On many occasions I broached the subject with Archie and Robert. They would shrug their shoulders as if it were of no real importance. I often wondered if they knew something that Helen and I did not.

To many in the community, the IRA was God and their actions gospel. I felt the brothers had accepted that their mum had somehow betrayed 'the cause' and had paid accordingly. When I spoke to old friends and neighbours of the family, I received the same response: the IRA would never have taken action against her unless it was necessary and justified. Conversations always ended with the same warning that I was treading on very iffy ground.

I had no idea how I was going to crack this nut but something had to end the torment. There were days and nights when Helen frightened the life out of me with her violent mood swings. I often asked her to consider counselling as I felt that she needed someone to help her cope with everything. I wasn't qualified to deal with her problems and when I suggested we contact victim support, she accused me of being 'no different to all the other bastards'. She was, of course, referring to all those who said that Jean's 'vanishing' was a figment of her imagination. I only wanted to help, but she trusted absolutely no one.

At this time, I was offered a job as a foreman in Holland and, given the difficulties we were experiencing, I jumped at the chance. I had always wanted to travel a bit, but more importantly, it wasn't just Helen who needed a break. Séamus McKendry PI was having no success finding the truth about Jean's disappearance, but was probably becoming a talking point in Republican circles for the wrong reasons. Apart from the initial bout of homesickness, I settled well and began learning the language. Whether through merit or luck, I managed to secure a salaried position, with house included, in the picturesque Baarn area.

Helen, needless to say, refused to consider taking up what was undoubtedly a superb opportunity to rear our children away from violence. She said that she wanted to be there if her mother, who might have been terribly traumatised by her abduction, had the courage to return home to her family. I knew in my heart that this was nonsense but I also sympathised with Helen and reluctantly left the job to be home with her and our children: Séamus, the eldest, was born in 1976, Kellyanne in 1979, Conor in 1982, Seán in 1984 and Sinéad in 1986.

On my return, I heard that two lads I knew had vanished from their homes. Rumour suggested that the pair had somehow upset the IRA and a 'nutting squad' (execution squad) had 'taken them out'. I decided to look up 'the queer fella' and ask him what he made of events. With a wry grin he told me this was the sort of thing that happened to people who pry into things that don't concern them, although he didn't actually admit that the IRA had been involved. For the first time, our conversation ended without my customary questions about Jean. Although it pained me deeply to admit defeat, I knew that all I could do now was sit back and hope that someday soon, someone would finally tell Helen the truth.

We decided to try to concentrate on our home and family, but every so often the depression returned and we would be back to square one. Arguments were prolific and I usually ended up going on a drinking session, regretting the day I returned from Holland.

In the following years, we saw less and less of Helen's family. With our own three, as well as Mickey still living with us, we didn't have room anymore to accommodate them.

Relations between the older family members had never been good and when we did see them, it would nearly always end up in some sort of sparring. Both grannies had, by now, died and the McConvilles were truly on their own.

Another aspect of Helen's behaviour that troubled me over the years revealed itself every time my family had some sort of party or function. Such occasions would almost certainly conclude with Helen causing a scene with either myself or one of my family. It appeared she couldn't stand seeing other families having fun together when hers had been so cruelly ripped apart. My wife had deep psychological problems that would have to be sorted out before I was driven to walking out. How we managed to remain together is a complete mystery. She was everything that I wanted in a woman until the moods set in and then, all of a sudden, I was sharing a home with a different, more aggressive and irrational person.

We stumbled through the next few years at a snail's pace. At my insistence, Jean's name was mentioned only if we read of some poor lass meeting a similar fate. I could always tell when Helen was thinking of her mum; she would go silent for days on end. When this happened, it was best to stay at work (I was working as a carpenter), take somebody's dog for a walk or simply hide in the pub. Even when Helen did manage to be in some sort of control, other factors would come into play to upset her again.

One of the people who abducted Jean took up residence just a few streets away and took great pleasure in sniggering at Helen at every opportunity. We were powerless to do anything about it; the woman made it quite clear that she still had the backing of the IRA. I never considered myself a violent person (I may have had weapons training but always refused to use them), but I have to admit that I regularly dreamed up ways of abducting one of the women involved and returning the 'hospitality' shown to Jean. Sometimes Helen and I were getting on well enough to go out for an evening together. Unfortunately, our night out would quite often be wrecked by some snide remark about Jean being a tout or a Loyalist's whore. I was getting desperate to find answers to this mystery that had confounded us for almost twenty years now.

The eighties had come and gone, little different to the bloody seventies that had preceded them. We found ourselves in the nineties and the slaughter continued. There was, however, a glimmer of hope on the horizon; Sinn Féin had finally come of age as a political party and was growing daily. It seemed that the struggle for unity was to be fought using politics instead of the gun. I had always dreamed that things would take this turn and I thought long and hard about taking an active role. I knew, however, that to do so would cause Helen unbelievable pain and so decided instead to watch from a distance.

A DEATH IN THE FAMILY

One morning in September 1992, I received a telephone call from Muckamore Abbey Hospital. In a very compassionate voice, a lady explained how Anne, Helen's eldest sister at thirty-nine, had died in the night from a stroke. I was immediately overcome with guilt and asked myself how we could have forsaken this poor woman all these years. She had harmed no one, yet we had allowed her to live out her years without so much as a visit.

I had often suggested to Helen that we visit Anne, but was told that Anne was prone to bouts of violence and so it wasn't a good idea.

I am one of eight children and have very close ties with all my siblings. I didn't understand how the McConvilles could neglect their sister in such a horrible fashion. My anger abated, however, when Helen arrived back from work that morning in tears. She had loved her sister; I was left in no doubt about that. She rushed to phone her brothers and sisters and a meeting ensued to discuss funeral arrangements.

Muckamore had offered to bury Anne in the Hospital grounds and I knew that everyone except Helen would agree to that. Her relief was obvious when I told her to lift the phone and make arrangements to have the body brought to our house for a wake. In the meantime, I contacted the prison where Robert now resided, guaranteeing (naïvely) to supervise him if they would consent to compassionate parole.

Helen babbled continually during the wake about her mother; she wondered whether or not Jean knew about the death. This was, after all, Jean's first child and Helen felt sure that this was the dawn of a new beginning. Anne would no longer be with them, but Helen was convinced that they would once again see their mother. Even as we carried the coffin to the cemetery, I was conscious of Helen panning the meagre cortege for a glimpse of the lady whose disappearance had caused so much sadness and despair.

It was not to be.

There were many suggestions as to why Jean, if still alive, was not at the funeral: if she were living across the water, she may not be aware of Anne's demise; perhaps she had heard but was terrified of coming to West Belfast; or maybe the senior Loyalist she resided with forbade it. The maybes would occupy our minds for the next many months.

When Jean never turned up to mourn her first born, Helen began to suspect that she was dead. Anne's headstone would have to wait, because Helen wanted to include her mum's name on it.

> ANNE McCONVILLE
> Died 29th September 1992 aged 39
>
> This plot is also reserved for our Mother Jean
> Disappeared by the Provisional IRA
> 7th December 1972
> Finally laid to rest here on the.......

I was relieved when I thought that she had at last succumbed to the rationale and accepted that her mother was dead. I had yearned for her to make this move for so many years. There would be no more need for the heartbreaking waiting for Jean's return; she could at last console herself with the knowledge that, like many others around us, she was a victim of the conflict.

I was fooling myself. Without the dust and bones of her mother's corpse, Helen would never allow herself to be called an orphan, never mind a victim.

There was another reason for her hesitation in going ahead with the inscription. If it were used, how would she look when a letter arrived informing her of the burial place of Jean McConville, who had demised in whatever year?

I realised that rather than help put Helen's mind at rest, Anne's death had, in fact, compounded her grief. Our days were now taken up with compiling lists of charitable organisations across the British Isles which might have knowledge of a terror-stricken young Belfast woman discovered destitute in 1972.

In the Summer of 1994, fearing for Helen's sanity and in an attempt to lift the cloud of despair that hung over us, I embarked on a pilgrimage to a club that was not unaccustomed to early hours clientele. While indulging in my usual alcoholic remedy, I was joined rather unexpectedly by none other than 'the queer fella'. After listening to my sad account of recent events and my wife's state of mind, he astonishingly promised me that, given a week or two, he would have news of some sort. He had just been released from Long Kesh and was very upbeat about the coming months, given the present political scenario. The dogs in the street were barking the herald of something new, and everyone was speculating about the content of the secret talks (that really weren't all that secret) taking place between the Provos and the Brits.

The next morning, I wondered at first if my encounter had been imagined. When I remembered our conversation, I could not establish if the tears I had shed were real or induced by Guinness. I castigated myself for appearing such a wimp. Either way, it had happened, but I said nothing to Helen, even though I wanted very much to do so.

I had placed impeccable trust in my old buddy and true to his word he called into my local a fortnight later. I was hesitant at first, this time he was not alone and his young colleague was a bundle of nerves. As suggested, I went for a short walk with the jumpy youth who amazed me by suggesting I pay a visit to Connolly House in Andersonstown, the Sinn Féin HQ. I asked rather awkwardly if I would not be presenting myself for execution.

I was to ask to speak to 'someone of authority' and to say nothing of himself or 'the queer fella'. They had agreed my inquiries over the years had been a genuine attempt to placate Helen and were not intended to undermine the Republican Movement.

I discussed the meeting with Helen, who became pretty excited about the proposed encounter. She also worried that something would go wrong, she didn't trust a hair on their heads. The Provo laying down of arms was imminent and I determined that there was no time like the present. That very afternoon I presented myself to 'someone of authority', who turned out to be someone I knew very well, a neighbour in fact. I told him the date of Jean's abduction, her age and other information I felt they might require. As I sat there, I was made to feel as if I were betraying the organisation by even suggesting their involvement in something like this. The more details he pencilled on the scrap of paper, the more annoyed he appeared. He didn't hold much hope, but said that he would see the information went to the right people and 'if I wanted' I could call back in three weeks. He emphasised the burdening workload the Movement was undertaking, which was a polite way of telling me to go away and not annoy them with trivial matters.

Back in my parent's home, Helen stood nervously waiting for my return. She almost expected me to have an address for her mother. There wasn't much cause for celebration, but at least we had had direct contact with 'the most sophisticated Guerrilla Army in the world' (as they are often referred to by the Press). I think Helen believed things would come to light, after all, we both knew the guy who had taken the details and, better still, he had originated from the Lower Falls area.

We prayed that the IRA would implement the promised cease-fire. When they did, we were far too selfish to join in the euphoria. The cessation of violence simply meant that we were less likely to be blown away (or at least that's what we were told by Republicans and Political commentators alike).

The three weeks had dragged in and with the proverbial butterflies flapping around, I once again entered Connolly House. As luck would have it, I was to see the person who I had first met. I immediately realised how pathetically naïve I had been when, to my surprise, he asked how he might help me. This guy had stood beside me on many occasions in the local and yet acted as if he didn't even remember our previous encounter. I began, once again, to stutter out the story of Jean before realising the futility of my situation and walking out. Fuming, I stormed off for home thinking that these people didn't give two damns for the likes of me, in fact, this man had stared right through me as I spoke.

Were we really stupid enough to believe that the IRA was going to admit to something that happened twenty-odd years ago or, more importantly, something that would be extremely damaging to them politically at this sensitive time?

Helen was devastated. I went back on the trail, foolishly hoping that, in the new environment, information would be more freely available. I soon found out that the IRA's system of wielding power and exerting control was intact. I also recognised that just because the Provos weren't killing didn't mean they couldn't. Although they were swapping the combat fatigues for suits, they were still a force to be reckoned with.

Helen talked incessantly about going to the newspapers, so that the world would know just how begrimed this little war had been. I genuinely believed this course of action would be suicidal. They might have tolerated my nosiness over the years, but they certainly wouldn't allow us to publicly embarrass them. There followed weeks of mental torture. Maybe Helen was right, if we went public, the IRA would have to think twice about harming us, they were, after all, on cease-fire. I found it a terrible quandary; there was no doubt in my mind that their actions were despicable, but there were many that I still classed as friends in the Republican Movement. I wondered if Jean had been an informer. If that were the case, then the volunteers ordered to punish her would have had no choice in the matter. Also, Helen and I both knew that in the unlikely event of someone being apprehended for her abduction, they would claim that, as a soldier in a war situation, they had to carry out orders.

It was finally decided to seek legal advice. The IRA and the Brits were in consultation and perhaps some sort of leverage could be employed to force the IRA to come clean. Apart from anything else, people were entitled to be compensated for the loss of a parent. Regardless of the amount, this would be official recognition that Jean McConville had existed. The chosen solicitor proved in the end to be rather uninterested. Jean was listed only as a missing person and when the solicitor did manage to discover the Police file, it consisted of two measly lines about a person going missing. To the solicitor's credit, he spoke to a friend in the BBC who enquired if she might call out to discuss the situation with us, but unsure of what to do we put her off.

Soon after this we had a visit from Fr Dennis Faul. Fr Faul (now Monsignor) has been an outspoken critic of the Provos since he attempted to halt the hunger strike in 1980. He talked at length about the brutality of the Provos and, I have to admit, I found him extremely difficult to fathom. He had been the prison chaplain in Long Kesh for quite some time and I wasn't sure on which side his bread was buttered. He convinced Helen that the only way to secure the truth was to go public. For his part, he promised to ask former prisoners if they had any knowledge of Jean's abduction, but said he didn't hold much hope of them owning up to such a horrific deed.

Within days, the lady from the BBC was back and, one way or another, she got Helen to agree to speak on Radio Ulster's *Talkback* programme. Too nervous to do the show live, Helen did a pre-recorded interview which was broadcast on 7 December 1994, the twenty-second anniversary of Jean's disappearance.

This interview was to change the dynamic of our search for truth, indeed, it was to change our lives.

THE CAMPAIGN

On the morning of the broadcast, we rose after a night of listening for cars and footsteps. The first task was to remove the planks that had been wedged behind the doors in case we had visitors in the night. Without speaking, we stumbled through the morning until the familiar theme tune of the *Talkback* programme could be heard. On separate radios, we listened in awe as this quietly-spoken voice recounted the horrors of her youth. I had heard this story a million times, so why all of a sudden was I reduced to tears? I was physically shaking and so was Helen. It was more than spotlight nerves, for we both knew we would now incur the wrath of the Republican Movement.

We assumed that Unionist listeners would have turned a deaf ear, thinking we probably deserved the horror just for being Catholics, and anyone from our own camp would simply despise us for shaming the Republican Movement. Instead, we listened gratefully to the feedback, caller after caller, both Nationalist and Unionist queued up to launch blistering attacks on the barbarians who had perpetrated the deed. Amazed that no one was attacking us, we felt relieved to know that there were decent human beings still living in Belfast and beyond. A call late that night from a good friend of ours really summed things up. The woman had been centrally involved in the IRA from childhood, while crying uncontrollably she professed her loathing at herself and her comrades for their combative methods. She said that she would be giving in her resignation first thing in the morning.

Calls from my own family were even more bewildering, they claimed to never having known the real story. My mother offered apologies for doubting Helen over the years, and another family member told how he had had to pull his car to the roadside as he listened to the programme, so shaken was he by the truth.

The McConville brothers soon arrived, but not to offer support. For years now, their children had believed that their granny had died from natural causes. Did she not know she had just put the whole family at risk? They said she was 'a selfish bitch'.

What chance had we of facing down the Provos when Helen's own clan were so opposed to securing the truth?

Following the old adage of safety in numbers, we made contact with other families whose relatives were missing and presumed dead as a result of the conflict. Now that we had publicised the issue, we would have to organise to protect ourselves. Rather reluctantly, family after family joined us and we agreed on a working name and *Families of the Disappeared* was born.

I chose the title to mirror the atrocities perpetrated by the Juntas in Latin America. As much as the Press needed a harrowing story, we needed a pretty high profile in order to protect ourselves. Soon every newspaper in the British Isles was reporting the story; our home became a virtual studio for the countless television and documentary crews who, quite simply, took over our lives.

On our first venture out since the radio broadcast, we were to get a taste of what was to come. Making our way to the bar to order a drink, I was pleased to notice folks stepping aside. The pleasure was soon turned to disgust when I realised that, rather than being mannerly, they were trying to get away from us. So this is what 'being sent to Coventry' meant. People we had known for years now turned their backs, it was pathetic and hurtful. We sipped our drinks, pretending to be relaxed when suddenly one courageous individual offered us their hand in a sympathetic manner. The 'freedom fighters' who would have us ostracised, were helpless to stop this show of solidarity. For once, common decency had prevailed, and we realised that some people were going to support us regardless of fear. Even so, we took a different route home and were constantly peering over our shoulders.

Petty harassment like this became the norm and we were often subjected to abuse and threats. I was expecting allegations about collusion with the Government and was not disappointed. Some asked how we could afford a new car? Others claimed to have been monitoring our movements and decided that British Intelligence had been paying us handsomely for our services. On more than one occasion I was told what a pleasure it would be when I got 'stiffed'.

By now, we had had numerous approaches from different organisations: political, civil and religious. We were loath to respond to any as we were adamant that we would not allow ourselves to be used as pawns. It was hard to refuse help as we badly needed some sort of financial help. We had a lot of expenses and even stamp costs were adding up. Petrol was also a drain on resources as we were driving all around the country meeting other families and politicians. Courting the media was still a nightmare, and the fact that they never put their hands in their pockets made it even worse. We could have asked for help, but felt that to do so would somehow tarnish what we were doing.

We had no idea about campaigning or lobbying and so I finally and reluctantly agreed to meet the FAIT (Families against Intimidation and Terror) group. They had been offering help for weeks, but knowing just how much this group were despised in Republican areas, it was a big decision. I knew that they were already talking with some of the other families and felt I had to interject to protect us all. It seems I moved at just the right time; I discovered their spokesman was already planning a merger. The assistance we received, in the form of computers and stationery, did little to win me over. Apart from the sincerity of members like Nancy Gracey and Sandra Peacock, I felt they had nothing to offer us. I also felt that the FAIT group had other motives for wanting to link our organisations. So-called 'punishment attacks' had abated somewhat since the cease-fire and we believed FAIT was just looking for some other reason to secure financing.

We would officially launch as an organisation on 26 June 1995 at the Linenhall Library in Belfast. We adopted a sky-blue ribbon as our emblem. Although a nerve-racking experience, it did give us an official platform from which we could apply for funding. We hoped that our financial worries were over.

Out of all the agencies I contacted, only one was prepared to offer assistance; a paltry £250, which was immediately eaten up by outstanding bills. It appeared partnership funding was available, which meant that we would have to be prepared to accept it in conjunction with other groups. This effectively ruled us out of the equation as we were not prepared to allow others to dictate our methods. Luckily, I was to receive some compensation for a motoring accident that had occurred a few years earlier and this tided us over and enabled me to attend the party conferences in Britain, where I stood alone begging for some support for our campaign.

An upside to these conferences was the existence of the 'fringe' activities, where I was given the opportunity to address the audiences. I had promised Sinn Féin a rough ride if they did not address the issue. Privately, their senior members would express the desire to have a resolution soon, but I felt they were being purely rhetorical. Gerry Adams had just recently been a guest on RTE's *Late Late Show* and presenter Gay Byrne did not miss the chance to question him about the plight of 'the disappeared'. Quite obviously embarrassed by the line of questioning, Adams promised to contact the families soon.

Some weeks later, a rather unwilling Mr Adams arrived at our door with his minder. He sat down and asked Helen what she knew of the events of December 1972. As she named those she knew to be involved in the abduction, he shook his head. He doubted very much if her information were authentic but would see if he could get someone from the IRA to pay us a visit. That 'someone' arrived a fortnight later, and only succeeded in upsetting us more with his arrogance. He looked at Helen like she were a piece of dirt on his shoe and as good as called her a liar. He said he knew the individuals she spoke of and claimed that they were all characters of impeccable standing. No sooner had he left the house than I had gone looking for 'the queer fella'. He couldn't believe the Movement could make such a hash of things and promised we would not have to endure his Nazi likes again.

Months passed with no communication at all with the Provos or Sinn Féin and it was only by chance that we saw Adams again. He had been out canvassing in a local shopping centre when I questioned him about our issue. He promised to call to see us again; but not for some time as he was extremely busy. 'Some time' was to become more than a year.

We chose this same venue for our first public show just a week later. Joined by Mrs Margaret McKinney (mother of Brian who disappeared in 1978) and our children, we nervously set up tables with reams of sheets for signature gathering. Feeling sure we would become a focus for abuse, I had made contingency plans for a quick getaway. As it happened, shoppers pushed past one another to sign their support for our campaign. The Sinn Féin party had failed, just a week earlier, to round up even a tenth of this crowd and we left that evening with thousands of signatures and a feeling of hope for the future.

A few months earlier, Helen had rather optimistically written to President Clinton. He not only had the decency to reply, but indeed showed great compassion. Proof that he had taken Helen's heartbreaking letter on board came that May when addressing world leaders at the Washington Investment Conference. In his speech he declared:

> Today there are families that have still not had the chance
> to grieve in peace, to visit the graves of their loved ones,
> to reunite after years of separation. It is time to allow
> families to be whole again.

Gerry Adams, who was sitting in the front row, nearly swallowed his pipe. Endorsement by the Clinton administration was more than we could have hoped for. Even with all the controversy surrounding his domestic life, the most important man in world politics had even taken the time to write to Helen on a personal level.

This is more than I can say for the leader of our largest Nationalist Party, the SDLP. Having received no reply to my first letter to John Hume, I wrote again, assuming I must have made some mistake with the address on the initial correspondence. Yet again, John ignored my plea to speak about the plight of 'the disappeared'. I could only surmise that, due to the precarious nature of his relationship with Adams, he didn't want to do anything that would rock the boat. His party colleague, Dr Joe Hendron, on the other hand, raised the issue at every given opportunity.

I never wanted it to turn into a 'them versus us' situation, but the only avenue open to me was to do as I had promised and embarrass Gerry Adams and his colleagues. I wished Sinn Féin nothing short of success, as it was better they be inside the Peace Process talking, than outside blowing the hell out of everything. 'The queer fella' rebuked me time and time again for my activities, which he claimed wouldn't be tolerated for much longer.

Our homelife was being badly affected by the situation. First our eldest son, and then our eldest daughter were assaulted on consecutive weekends for being the children of 'anti-Republican scum'. This kind of abuse could not be tolerated. I am every bit as Irish as the next but I cannot condone the killing of civilians as a means of achieving independence, or anything else for that matter.

Not a day went past when Sinn Féin didn't release a Press statement condemning some human rights abuse or other. This really annoyed me as we were practically prisoners in our own home. This hypocrisy couldn't have been highlighted better than by an article that was faxed to me by a journalist friend. On reading the piece, I concluded it a worthy account of the harrowing disappearances perpetrated by Shillingo and his military cohorts in Argentina. They were responsible for the deaths of thousands of people they considered to be agitators. Imagine my horror when I read the footnote, only to discover that the article was from that week's *An Phoblacht* (Republican News). Just what right had these people to condemn, when they were guilty of identical crimes here? To make matters worse, Helen noticed the date of the publication; 7 December 1995, the twenty-third anniversary of her mother's disappearance.

My days were filled with meeting human rights groups and politicians, attending conferences or generally annoying somebody. We had started and there was no turning back, in fact, I was beginning to enjoy it. I had been suffering excruciating back pain since a few off-duty members of Her Majesty's Army had used me as a football in London in 1989 when I was there on a carpentry job. It had effectively rendered me incapable of work, but playing the 'caped crusader' now gave me a purpose in life. I relished being given the opportunity to meet ambassadors, film stars and the like, but I still loathed having to appear in front of cameras. My remnant of a brain had been on reserve tank for years now and it was invigorating to speak to people with intelligence.

Although I despised being filmed, I was becoming fascinated by the whole media thing and would often annoy producers with my unwelcome input. We realised that we were only important to them in terms of the story, but having media coverage was the best way to ensure that the world became aware of the disappearance of Jean and the other twelve or so individuals in our files.

Only on one occasion could I say they overstepped the mark. A major current affairs programme company had sent over a researcher to try and coax me into naming, on air, the names of those that we knew had been involved in Jean's abduction. I arranged to meet him in *Crown Liquor Saloon* ('the Crown' bar) in Belfast, where I think the buying of a pint of Guinness was supposed to persuade me to start talking. The moron proceeded to produce a very curious looking mobile phone and placed it right in front of me. I, of course, asked what it was, and he replied that it was only a phone and he had put it there because he was hearing impaired. To cut a long story short, the meeting ended with me crushing it underfoot and leaving him to finish two pints.

All the 'doubting Thomases' who had said we would never be able to get the campaign off the ground were proved patently wrong. We had succeeded in letting the world know just how grotesque the past thirty years of war had really been. We still stuck to our initial stance of not allowing anyone to use us for their own ends, but that didn't mean I couldn't use them. For instance, I wanted 'the disappeared' issue raised in the European Parliament. John Hume had made himself (for whatever reason) unavailable, so I thought nothing of employing the good Doctor, Ian Paisley, to further my aims. Arch-bigot he may well be, but he has a huge mouth and is not reticent about using it. This was a basic human rights issue, above politics and creed, and I knew when I left his office that day that I had evoked a measure of sympathy in him. Jim Nicholson, the Official Unionist MEP, also promised to do everything in his power to ensure we were not forgotten and, like Paisley, felt sure there were similar cases in the Loyalist camp. Although I have made extensive enquiries over the years, I have not discovered a disappearance that could be attributed to Loyalist paramilitaries. It appears this is strictly a Republican phenomenon. I also discovered that this was not a new form of terror; during the Irish Civil War it appears it was common practice. *Police Casualties in Ireland 1919–21* by Richard Abbot (a serving member of the RUC) clearly illustrates that the term 'Bog-job' in reference to an IRA secret burial has been in use for quite some time.

For every battle we won, it appeared there was one to be lost. Amnesty International, who had championed cases (including Republican ones) over the years had always commanded my respect, but I felt they let me down badly when I asked them to intervene. They appeared to be only interested in injustices that were perpetrated by the security forces. Both Helen and I came away from our meeting with their representatives feeling we had done something terribly wrong by speaking about the IRA in such a manner. Bianca Jagger, the actress, left us feeling the same when we met her in her capacity as representative of a human rights group. I had taken a camera that day in the hope of having a snapshot for my pals to drool over, but was so taken back by her indifference that I pushed it to the bottom of my bag.

Was it okay for independence groups to carry out atrocities? I was beginning to wonder. If a member of the so-called Security Forces (who I have never had time for), even as much as blinked, there was a furore and demands for independent inquiries; yet a young mother of ten could just vanish off the face of the earth. There was definitely something wrong here.

When we felt rejected by these groups, it would be the ordinary folk who regularly stopped us in the street that bolstered our morale. We were, by now, so often on the television that we were recognised no matter where we went. For every one who doled out a mouthful of abuse, there were fifty others who would shake our hands and offer to pray that someday soon we would have a resolution. These sincere individuals really did make our sufferance worthwhile.

It's as well I possess a warped sense of humour as not everyone who wished us well did so sincerely. While I was having a pint one night, a guy who I knew to be sympathetic to the Provos bent my ear about others not doing enough to help me locate the bodies of 'the disappeared'. He promised to do something there and then. He left, leaving me suspiciously perplexed, only to return some minutes later with a garden spade. The next morning we discovered that some people were prepared to do more than sneer at our actions. Our car had been the target of someone's imbecilic hatred; the doors and roof had been systematically kicked and battered. For the first time we seriously considered getting out of Belfast.

This notion of voluntary exile was to become an important consideration to protect the children when, later the same week, an old mate with a face chock-full with guilt told us how, at a recent pow-wow with his peers, it was suggested I be 'taken out'. He went on to say that he had told them shooting me would be counter-productive during the cease-fire and would go against the general shift in Republican thinking. The response he received was that no-one had mentioned shooting; an 'accident' could easily be arranged. A car could mount a kerb, or a pub brawl could be staged. I have been stubborn all my life, refusing to be corralled by anyone, and I wasn't going to start backing away now.

MAKING WAVES

I continued to have a pint in my local and insisted on using the popular black taxis to go about my business. These black hackney cabs had been purchased to transport the people of West Belfast in the absence of buses etc. that were regularly being burnt out. I was doing something to ease my wife's agony, something that anyone with an ounce of respect for humanity would have done and I was going to continue despite the risks. Seán, a guy who I had been friendly with for some time, called me aside one day. He had not spoken to me since I joined Helen publicly. He enquired as to just what it would take to shut me up. I told him I had no intention of stopping until I had established exactly what had become of Jean McConville. 'If I could discover that', he asked, 'would you shut your fucking trap?!' I knew I was making waves in the right places; this man had been a serious operator in his day and had the bullet wounds to prove it. I repeated my desire to establish the truth but declined to commit myself to his ultimatum.

A fortnight later, the hairs on the back of my neck stood upright when he told me in an emotionless tone: 'We stiffed her, go and tell her that, and fuck off.' I knew fine well by his demeanour that he had indeed spoken to someone in the know.

I had created an audio journal of the eerie discourse on my cassette recorder but didn't want Helen to hear it. When Helen went silent for the next couple of days, I realised that she had found the tape. I apologised profusely for being so amateurish and leaving the accursed tape where she might find it. She was, in a sense, glad to hear at last something to explain her mum's absence. She had known in her heart for years that they had killed her. Knowing who had given me the chilling information, she, like myself, had no doubt about its authenticity.

About this time, groups and individuals alike were making representation to the International Body on Decommissioning, headed by Senator George Mitchell. I wrote, asking if he would consider meeting our delegation even though we had no real interest in the decommissioning argument. If the guns were silent, then we weren't particularly bothered if they were surrendered or not. Senator Mitchell, decent gentleman that he is, obliged, and we set about figuring out how we might get him to discuss 'the disappeared'. It was quite easy in the end, I simply told him our priority was the decommissioning of the bodies that the IRA had so heinously dumped in unmarked graves. The Senator and his panel were obviously very moved by what they heard, but I think also a little bemused by our craft. When we read their report, we very happily discovered the issue of the bodies of the disappeared to be included.

I had no doubt annoyed the Republican Movement with my persistent intrusions. Instead of being threatened half a dozen times daily, it now seemed as though the tirade of abuse flowed continuously from morning to night. We were literally looking over our shoulders. Our children had supported us from day one and often remarked that if anything should happen to us, they would continue to fight for justice. One Christmas we held a vigil outside City Hall in Belfast. They endured sub-zero temperatures with us for more than twelve hours when even the other families had let us down. They were the offspring of Séamus and Helen alright and were not going to bow to terror.

As quickly as we had been thrown into the spotlight, we found ourselves out of it. The Provos had spectacularly ended their cessation of violence by blowing the hell out of Canary Wharf in London, taking two civilian lives in the process. We were now relegated to doing the odd religious documentary for foreign viewing. It was nerve-racking being out on our own; it was a time of despondency and fear. With the resumption of killing, we knew that we were targets, perhaps more so now than previously. It looked like 'the disappeared' had truly disappeared and become mere archive material.

Meanwhile, we had a visit from a senior Sinn Féin official. He might have thought his appearance to be a surprise, but we had been expecting someone. The previous night, a reporter from *The Scotsman* newspaper had phoned to say that a senior Sinn Féin member had told him that an announcement was imminent on the whereabouts of those who had vanished. I had managed to obtain a copy of the newspaper early that morning and I smiled inwardly as the 'Shinner' took great lengths to warn me against media speculation; he totally rubbished the paper (that I was not supposed to have seen). I concluded that this was the 'senior source' that had spoken to the journalist.

I figured he had had his knuckles rapped by his leadership for giving out such information prematurely. Incredibly, he went on to enquire about rumours he had heard of harassment to our family and asked us to report any such incidents so that they might 'sort out' the perpetrators. We found it difficult to keep straight faces. Before leaving, he told me to remove the name of Crossmaglen man Charlie Armstrong from our files. 'Everyone knows he was a suicide', he told me. I retorted, 'Wouldn't it be convenient to say all the cases were suicide victims?'

Our two youngest, Seán and Sinéad are two years apart in age and have their birthdays on consecutive days. Although money was scarce, in November of 1995 Helen decided to take them to the local McDonalds for a bit of a treat. Whilst standing in the queue, she was aware of a commotion behind.

'Mummy it's you that woman's shouting at', said the youngest. Helen turned around to see a face from the past. It was none other than the female 'volunteer' who had remained unmasked during her mother's abduction. The wretched creature was screaming about being fed up with harassment. The tirade continued long after her equally wretched husband had dragged her from the building. That night we were left to ponder the source of her torment, it couldn't have been the Police, for we hadn't spoken to them with regard to individuals who might have had involvement. So it must have been the IRA themselves.

This contradicted what the IRA, and indeed Adams, had told us, just a few months previously. When I had asked (sarcastically) about extracting information from those individuals who were known to have participated, Gerry suggested: 'We just don't do things that way anymore.' I told him if they were time-honoured methods, then surely they should be continued.

In all honesty, I was glad. No matter how much hatred I harboured for this 'ideological whore', I really wouldn't have relished knowing, that in some way or other, I had a part in subjecting her to the injustice of a backstreet court.

She had lowered her shield, and any further utterances would only serve to drop her in it. We took pleasure in knowing we were being successful at strumming the heart strings of those involved. From day one, we reckoned that time would lure out the facts. This individual, supposedly living a normal life in Twinbrook, was cracking at the seams and we were sure that someday she would provide us, or maybe even the powers that be, with Jean's itinerary that fateful 7 December.

The bolt-hole that I had been seeking for some time had presented itself. There was a small condemned cottage lying vacant in the area where I was born. Immediately, I went to work on Helen and the kids. She was too enthusiastic and I guessed correctly that she just wanted me to get out of Belfast. The children, abused as they had been, preferred to stay put. They claimed they could face up to the odd beating. The question was, when would a bit of harassment become a murder inquiry?

Living in the 'sticks' was no panacea for what we'd been through, but it certainly enabled us to get a full night's sleep. At least now we could hear a car, even if it was a mile away. In Belfast we could hear cars all the time and so it was difficult to ascertain if they were approaching our house. We knew fine well that the Provos would have no trouble tracing us if they so desired, but at least now we had some distance between us.

Just a few weeks after moving to our 'secret' hideaway in 1996, we received an invite from the American Consulate to attend their 4 July celebration. A break was in order and we decided to avail of the opportunity to chin-wag with the numerous VIPs who would be there. Midway through the evening, Alex Maskey of Sinn Féin enquired about my health. I said it would be much better if they got their act together and let us bury our dead, one of which was a cousin of his own. Appearing sympathetic, he said that he and his colleagues were doing everything in their power to sort things out. Then, with a sickly grin, he told me that the house I had moved to was in a lovely spot and commented on how convenient it must be to have my parents living just down the road. They had been doing their homework and he was letting me know it.

For all the initial enthusiasm, Helen hated the damp-ridden little hovel to which I had brought her. Most of her days were to be taken up driving back to Belfast to visit friends. It would be the beauty of a country spring that finally persuaded her and the children that this could and would be a place they would grow to love. The periodic cleaning of the shotguns, did somehow diminish the tranquillity, but we always had to be prepared.

THE DISAPPEARED

If the newspapers were to be believed, then I wasn't doing my job properly.

'Twenty bodies buried on Black Mountain', cried one Sunday paper. Other papers put the number disappeared at fifty. To date we had received information on seven. I decided it was time to correct these figures and requested a meeting with the RUC. I insisted on having the interview recorded; this was due to my inbuilt distrust of anything to do with the Police or Army. They had in their possession quite an extensive list of people who had gone astray during what they like to call 'the troubles' (three-and-a-half thousand citizens killed and they insist on naming it after some domestic between a husband and wife).

They were pretty certain that I knew the names of people who were involved in some of these vanishing acts. If I were prepared to enlighten them, they could make their files accessible to me. The truth was, the RUC knew very little about the individuals who had purportedly gone astray, or, as it happened, chose to know nothing. I was soon to realise that some of the people I was trying to locate were actually people I despised all my life (without even knowing them). It was an awful realisation; I, Séamus McKendry, who despised those who would betray their own people, was actually campaigning on their behalf. Serious thought would have to be given to my *modus operandi* from here on. I left that day with the names of twelve people who had been reported missing through paramilitary action to the Police.

Some of these individuals were undoubtedly killed for having allegiance to the crown forces. I had to take myself back to the early seventies and imagine just what I would have thought had I been sitting on a panel of 'justice'. I had no doubt that as an impressionable youngster I would have sanctioned the death penalty for their treasonous activities, but the word or implication from someone like me should never be enough to send someone to their death. I recalled serious debates we had had in my early 'revolutionary' days about miscarriages of justice, how we had castigated the British judicial system for sending people (especially Irish people) to their deaths on the flimsiest of evidence. In my early training the emphasis had been on consultation; never get too far ahead of yourself without first consulting those closest to the intended action. This maxim echoed in my head when I decided to represent all of those who had 'disappeared', regardless of what they had done.

I vividly recall having a pint with the editor of the *Sunday World*, Jim McDowell. 'Listen kid', he said 'I've got to admire your guts for taking the stance you have, but you're seriously going the right way about getting a bullet in the head by having Nairac on your list.' Captain Robert Nairac had been an undercover soldier operating in South Armagh, amongst other places, when the IRA rumbled him in May 1976.

Where did we even begin? The corpses of twelve persons, assumed executed for whatever reason, had to be discovered. The obvious thing to do was to talk to their families in order to ascertain their last known movements and acquaintances. This was going to be no easy task as some of these people were staunch Republican supporters and believed their relative had transgressed and therefore deserved to be executed.

A late night phone call from a priest was to set the ball rolling, at least in our own case. He said he had information concerning Jean and wanted us to agree to meet him the following day in a Belfast hotel.

After the obligatory coffees, he said that two former members of the Provisionals had been to see him and were willing to tell him what they knew about Jean's abduction, in return for some cash. Before I could utter the words 'you didn't', he admitted he had. Surely whatever he was now to tell us would have to be taken with a pinch of salt. He admitted it may have been foolish to pay up front, but he was determined to make sure that Jean McConville would have a Christian funeral.

Shovelling out money to every idiot that was down on his luck was not the way to acquire genuine information. As it was, one of these guys claimed that as a volunteer back in the early seventies, he had been ordered to keep an eye out whilst his comrades interrogated a woman in the bedroom of a house in Beechmount Grove. He claimed the woman, whom he now knew through media coverage to have been Jean, was eventually taken from the house by four men. They returned without her just a few minutes later. He had not heard any shots and wasn't aware of a car or similar transport in the area. The priest then produced a sketch map of the area and the names of three of the interrogation team, all of whom were known to me and had a history in the IRA. Just how reliable the map and names were we didn't know. The information would have been easier to believe had no money crossed hands.

Through a source close to the Housing Executive, I was able to establish that the name of the householder which was supplied was indeed correct. She had been living alone with her children while her husband, a Provo, was serving a sentence in Long Kesh. On the other hand, one of the interrogators, whom they very clearly implicated, couldn't possibly have been involved as he was interned at the time.

Could they have made the whole thing up, just to get a few measly pounds? Their story did have a ring of truth when I compared the details with those given a year back by the Provo who said they had 'stiffed her'.

Whether true or not, we travelled to the address given straight away. It had been lying derelict for some years now and the windows were bricked up. This place stank of evil and we were pretty sure some aspects of his story were correct.

Willing to try anything to shed light on the mystery, Helen went to see a well-known and respected clairvoyant, who absolutely astounded us by relating practically the same story, even down to describing the area of Beechmount. We had no doubt in our minds that the grim-looking hovel we discovered had played some part in the cruel demise of her mother.

There was little enough on the case of Jean, but the others left us even more bewildered. The earliest disappearances were of two lads from the Falls Road, Kevin McKee and Seamus Wright, both of whom went missing from their homes in the Summer of 1972. McKee was in fact the nephew of Billy McKee, Officer Commanding of the Belfast Brigade. The chances of extracting some information from this quarter were always going to be difficult. Helen, through a mutual friend, was invited for a girl's night out with some of the McKee clan and was quite surprised to find that they wanted nothing more than to lay their loved one to rest. They talked at length about Kevin in his younger days but wouldn't be drawn on the months prior to his disappearance. They told Helen that they had nothing but respect for her for the courage she had shown in standing up to the IRA. These people were in an impossible dilemma, they agonised over the loss, just as anyone else would, but could not express their sorrow because of the family ties with Republicanism.

The IRA was running scared at the time of the disappearances, lax recruitment practices had left them vulnerable to infiltration and the British Secret Service had a field day. The scale of panic in the IRA ranks was evident by the number of its own members found tortured and killed. Indeed they were responsible for more volunteers being killed than the Army, Police and Loyalists put together.

I have often wondered if the disappearance of Jean later that year was attributed to the same paranoia. We have established that at least a dozen unmarried or widowed young women were picked up and interrogated by the Provos. All but Jean were allowed to return to their families after a day or two. A phone call inviting me to come into town, promised to shed a little more light. 'The queer fella' was sitting on his own when I arrived in *The Liverpool Bar*. We talked generally for a while before he went on to tell me that he had heard from a very good source that they had, unintentionally, killed Jean. A plastic bag had been placed over her head to frighten her and (given the state of her health at the time) she took a panic attack and died. This all made a lot of sense to me. If she died in their hands, they would not have been able to just drop her body somewhere, as too many people knew who had abducted her. The only option open to her captors was to make sure the body would never be found.

This suited everyone, except the family of course, who would have to endure the stigma of having a 'whore' for a mother. When I left 'the queer fella', I knew he was deeply troubled about the whole affair. I believe he was left questioning his loyalty to the organisation.

In 1974, another Seamus Wright, no connection to the one above, and his friend John McIlroy disappeared on their way to work in Andersonstown. Try as I might, I found it impossible to gather even the most basic information on them. One evening, in a bar, I was approached by two Republicans from Andersonstown. They enquired if I knew anything of the missing pair and then proceeded to roar with laughter and walk off. I felt this was their way of telling me that I could pry all I wanted, but would never resolve the mystery.

At least two other men would also disappear the same year. The first was Patrick Mooney who was feared dead when his bloodstained car was found several miles away from the place where he had just picked up the firm's payroll. His family had contacted us, obviously fearing he had been abducted by paramilitaries. In 1996, on the advice of the Police, I removed his name from our literature when I was informed of his being alive and well and living a quite comfortable life in the south of England.

No such explanation was forthcoming for twenty-four-year-old Brendan Megraw, from Twinbrook estate. A motorcycle enthusiast, he was known as a quiet reserved type with no political aspirations. In their first year of marriage, when Brendan and wife Marie were expecting their first child, a group of armed men rushed into their flat and proceeded to force Marie to a chair whereupon she was injected with some unknown substance. Hazily, she recalls a commotion and Brendan being dragged out. Pulling herself to the window she remembered seeing a sporty-type Volkswagen speeding away.

This was definitely not your average abduction. Why did they deem it necessary to drug Marie? Who was adequately trained to administer the drug to a woman who was six months pregnant? I considered this to be too clinically executed to be the work of the local Provos and immediately suspected the SAS or a similar undercover team. Brendan, I later learned, had been a witness to the killing of Andersonstown Republican Jack McCartan. Was this one way of making sure his testimony would never be heard? Things became even more confused when I discovered that Brendan had been an acquaintance of twenty-two-year-old Myles 'Fred' McGrogan, whose activities as an agent provocateur led to his capture and execution by the IRA at Colin Glen Wood,

Hannastown, in April 1977. Indeed Brendan had even attended the funeral. Later, when shown family photographs, I realised I had known this lad myself. Belfast is truly only a village.

The disappearance of young Columba McVeigh on Halloween night 1975 must rank as one of the dirtiest deeds ever perpetrated during the conflict. Just seventeen years old, this wee fella would have been described as 'slow' by any standards. It is widely believed that the handful of ammunition recovered by the British Army in his home, had in fact been placed there by McVeigh on the instruction of the British Army. This youngster became an unwilling participant in an intricate yet bungled attempt by military intelligence to infiltrate the Provisionals in Co. Tyrone and discover how IRA personnel were able to flee to the Republic. The leniency of the four-month suspended sentence only served to harden the suspicions of the already alert IRA. Columba went to Dublin to stay with a brother and had been happily employed as a painter when homesickness set in and he returned to Donaghmore, where a 'death squad' was waiting. He had transgressed; the fact that he was innocently drawn into a web of intrigue by the hidden faces from Whitehall mattered little and he was taken across the border and executed. His body was thrown into a ready-made bog grave.

The McVeigh family, through Fr Denis Faul, have pleaded many times for the IRA to come clean on the whereabouts of his remains but have so far been ignored. Fr Faul summed things up when he described the teenager as a young and innocent victim of both sides and a victim of the 'whole sick society' that is Northern Ireland.

I still to this day have no idea what criteria are used to determine whether a victim should vanish or be discovered on some remote back road. Certainly the 'botched affairs', like Jean's death, had to be hidden, but why, for instance, was young Columba McVeigh's body not left for his parents to bury. Surely it makes sense to show the dead person if your aim is to dissuade others from informing.

Twenty-two-year-old Brian McKinney and eighteen-year-old John McClory, Bru and Bugsy as they were known to everyone, including myself, would join the list of the disappeared in 1978.

If ever I am asked to give an example of people who invited hassle from the IRA, then these two fitted the bill. I had chummed around with them and their colleagues as a fifteen-year-old. Their acquaintances would consist of members of IRA and INLA as well as your average crook on the lookout for easy money. Society had crumbled since the start of the conflict; there were no police patrols or 'bobbies' on the beat and this gang, among others, capitalised on this fact. Weapons would be 'borrowed' regularly by those who were also in the paramilitaries, and used by the likes of Bugsy and Bru to rob anyone they could. The guns would then be returned to their hiding place and the mercenaries would have a whale of a time drinking and partying with the ill-gotten gains.

The gang overstepped the mark when they carried out a robbery at the *Clubhouse* bar on the Glen Road. This establishment was a known Provisional haunt and it is hard to believe that they were foolish enough to go near it. Soon afterwards, the two lads were pulled in by the local unit of Provos, who were more interested in where the gun had been acquired than the actual robbery. McKinney had been identified as the one who had actually held the weapon and so the two boys felt sure they would be kneecapped. It is almost certain that McClory played no part in the robbery itself, but he did share in the spoils. Miraculously, the two were released unharmed after a couple of day's interrogation. I was later told that this happened because far too many had witnessed their abduction. Something didn't ring true about this. Firstly, they were well-known rogues, so it would have come as no surprise to hear they had been kneecapped. Secondly, the taking of IRA guns for personal gain was like signing your own death warrant. Yet gang members who were also Provisionals were not harmed in any way. I believe they were allowed to go back to their families so that they could be monitored for activities that were suspected to be more serious. The McKinney family, on hearing about the robbery, gave back what would have been Brian's cut of the take and made him apologise to the publican. They believed this would be the end of it all.

On the morning of 25 May 1978, Bugsy failed to arrive at the Mary Peter's Athletic Track for work. His buddy Bru turned up at Bernagh Drive to commence his work as a gardener, but soon afterwards was seen getting into a car and heading off. They would never be seen again. Stories abounded about their lives as bank and security van robbers; from Dublin to Acapulco, heists are attributed to 'Bugsy and Bru'. A £1000 reward offered at the time, was never taken up.

A more sinister version of events was told to Bugsy's sister in a drinking club some years later. One of his old buddies bragged about how the ill-fated pair had been killed for anti-social activities and secretly buried close to their homes. From my own investigations, I discovered that one of the IRA squad was willing to speak about the 1978 abductions. He claimed that the lads were held in a third-storey flat in Lenadoon, where they were beaten and interrogated. He went on to claim that, fearing they were soon to be executed, McClory rushed past his captors and jumped through the window, falling thirty feet to the ground below. He was pursued and, failing to stop, shot in the back. He would die instantly from his injuries and, as there was no option left to them, they took McKinney out and killed him also. My source went on to explain how a small van was commandeered and the lifeless bodies were taken to nearby Glen Road Housing Estate, where they were buried in the foundations of partly constructed houses. He described in minute detail how they carried the tarpaulin-wrapped bodies to the hurriedly excavated grave. This man went so far as to actually take me to the scene, but with the passage of time could not be precise about the location of the grave.

Mary McClory, John's mother, has, on many occasions, implored Alex Maskey, a senior Sinn Féin member in Belfast and cousin of her own, to assist in the search for her son. To date, however, he has been either unable or unwilling to help.

The abduction and subsequent death of Captain Robert Nairac is probably the best documented of 'the disappeared', but I feel it will also prove to be the most difficult to resolve. The fact that he was in the British Army, tends to distance him from any sympathies that might be out there. Nairac, from a devout Catholic family in Gloucester, was seconded to the SAS from the Coldstream Guards in January 1976 and almost immediately took up residence in the South Armagh region. His brief included the recruitment of informers in the staunchly Republican area.

In May 1977, while posing as a Belfast Republican and singing rebel songs in the *Three Steps Inn* at Drumintee, he was confronted by a group of local men, at least one of whom was a member of the IRA. After a particularly savage beating, he was dragged to a car and taken to Ravensdale Forest where it is believed he was shot dead after a botched interrogation.

The abduction of a leading operative from the SAS was, or rather should have been, a major propaganda coup for the IRA. Instead, they were left with a dead soldier who wasn't able to tell them anything about undercover activity in the area. In an attempt to make the best of a bad thing, the IRA pretended that the soldier was still alive and providing them with valuable information. For fear that his body, which was being sought by the Police and Army on both sides of the border, might be discovered, and therefore ruin the ruse, the local IRA commanded that it be disposed of in such a manner as to ensure it would never be found. Indeed, if popular opinion is to be believed, then his body never will be.

An acquaintance of mine from Co. Louth, who became disillusioned with the IRA and their move towards a political solution, confided to me that the often quoted 'mincer theory' was indeed correct. He claimed to have been 'in a position to know' at the time of Nairac's demise. The local meat processing plant, staffed by many with Republican affiliations, became the macabre destination for Nairac's beaten body, which he claims became animal fodder. There are many equally fantastic stories surrounding the whereabouts of the soldier's remains, but I have to say, knowing my acquaintance's history, I am prepared to accept his grisly account of affairs.

Whilst updating the list of victims, I had a visit from an old associate, a veteran of the conflict in fact and a staunch Republican from his childhood in the 1940s. I was quite amazed when he asked why a member of his own family was not listed in our literature.

Not having a clue to whom he was referring, I invited him to elaborate. Danny McIlhone, he offered, whereupon I interrupted: 'Sure I knew Danny well, his body had been found where they killed him, hadn't it?' He told me that I was wrong and that his body has never been recovered. The rumour factory was alive and well. He went on to tell me that the family had given him a hard time over Danny's disappearance. He had been well placed in the Movement and could therefore find out for them, they hoped. On his release from prison, he did indeed make enquiries at headquarters, but was politely told to mind his own business. Putting himself in the firing line he later returned to ask again, and this time was asked: 'What are you getting all hyped up about, sure didn't he get a nice wee send off in the Wicklow mountains?' This response from the Provisionals was relayed to the family, who were at least able to begin to face the fact that Danny was dead.

Having moved out of Andersonstown at the time of his disappearance, I was only able to pick up snippets of information. The story I'd heard was that Danny had been seen getting into a Special Branch car at the top of Bingham Drive, close to his home. It was therefore not much of a surprise to hear the Provos had him; rumour is all that was needed to 'take someone out' in war ravaged West Belfast.

A young reporter friend decided to call at the McIlhone's to verify the story, but was told (as I forewarned she would be) that Danny was alive and well and working abroad. The family had been told in no uncertain terms that Danny was dead, yet chose a story that would save the Republican Movement any embarrassment. I can only say that my family would always take priority over my politics, but then who am I to judge?

So many of 'the disappeared' were suspected to have been handed over to the South Armagh units for interrogation and execution, that it came as no surprise when we were asked to look into cases from Crossmaglen, the Republican heartland. The first was that of Gerald Anthony Evans, aged twenty-four, from Rathview Park in the town. Described as a family lad, he resided with his parents and brothers, who say he was anything but a troublemaker and indeed took great pleasure in telling the local Provos where to go. Unlike many young men in the area, the armed struggle held no mystique for him, and he was regularly in confrontation with 'The Boys'. Last seen on 27 March 1979 trying to hitch a lift home on the roadside outside Castleblaney, Gerald's whereabouts are a mystery to this day. Locals feel he overplayed a macho image and was killed by renegade Republicans.

At fifty-six, Mr Charlie Armstrong, a neighbour of Gerald's, was the eldest of the victims. He left his home at 10 a.m. on 16 August 1991 to collect a neighbour for Sunday morning mass, as was his regular routine. He never arrived at the neighbours, but his unlocked grey Datsun car was discovered across the border at the Adelphi cinema in Dundalk that night.

At least four witnesses had seen Charlie that morning, his driving licence was missing and the only fingerprints found in the car were his own. This was the individual whose name the Provos had told me to remove from my files. They were convinced he had taken his own life, yet when a search of the surrounding countryside was launched for Charlie, local Republicans were noticeable by their absence. To be fair though, in this tightly-knit community, people are extremely reluctant to speak out or even look near anything that could be construed as compromising a Provo operation.

The fifteenth case to come to light was that of Seamus Ruddy from Newry in Co. Down.

Seamus first came to the attention of the authorities back in 1978 when he was arrested in a camper van packed with weapons and explosives on the Greek-Turkish border.

The son of a Newry Labour Councillor, the academically astute Ruddy became the national organiser of the Irish Republican Socialist Party (IRSP), the political wing of the INLA, and editor of *The Starry Plough*. He was particularly prominent in the hunger strike campaigns of 1980-81 and went on the run to Paris after a volatile shake up within the INLA in 1983, when he publicly dammed the organisation for the direction it was taking.

In Paris, he seemed to have settled well. He established the Irish Association for Cultural Affairs and began teaching English at a private school. Although there were many IRSP sympathisers in the city at the time, his girlfriend, Cecilia Moore, maintains he kept himself very much to himself. He was last seen going to meet up with 'friends' of old in May of

1985 and it is accepted that after a dispute with these 'friends' he was murdered and secretly buried.

By no means were these fifteen the only individuals to disappear. In 1973, the Provisionals kidnapped the German industrialist and envoy to Northern Ireland, Thomas Neidermeyer. The operation became unstuck when he died, probably of a heart attack. The industrialist, now dead, was of no financial use to the organisation and his body was quickly hidden in Colin Glen Wood. It remained there until the arrest of one of the kidnappers whose information led to the body being recovered from a rubbish tip in the wood on 11 March 1980.

In the same year, police responding to a tip-off were amazed to discover a brand new coffin lying across the seats of a brown Cortina which was abandoned at the Buncrana Road border crossing. The car had been hijacked earlier in the Creggan area of Derry. The coffin contained the remains of thirty-three-year-old Patrick Duffy, a father of seven from the Creggan. The Derry man had disappeared from a bar in Buncrana, Co. Donegal almost two weeks previously, and there had been strong speculation that the Provos had murdered him. This was confirmed in a letter to his wife, Margaret, in which the IRA claimed Duffy admitted to being a paid informer for Army Intelligence and the RUC Special Branch. Mrs Duffy went on to make a public appeal for the return of her husband's body so that he might receive a proper Christian burial. The inquest later told how the body had been shot and immersed in water for some length of time and that it had been sprinkled in a substance, probably lime. My source claims that a leading Sinn Féin man from Derry played a pivotal role in the return of the body.

On 2 May 1979 a manhunt was started when the burnt-out van of post office worker Sean Murphy, a twenty-three-year-old from Cullyhanna, was discovered at Tullydonnel, South

Armagh. Two days later, a very relieved family friend received a call from Mr Murphy saying he was alive and well and in the Irish Republic. He was to return home in December 1981 where arson charges awaited him. He never made the court appearance and the RUC believed he was hiding out in the South once again. On 17 July, Dundalk Gardaí discovered the remains of Murphy in his car, which had been dredged from the harbour. Once again it was believed that local Republicans were somehow involved.

In 1983, Fr Denis Faul made an impassioned plea to the Provisionals in South Down to say whether or not they had killed the Bryansford father of four, Eugene Simmons. He was last seen on New Year's Day 1981 leaving a party willingly with some men in the area. Fr Faul went on to say that Simmons had been detained in Gough Barracks for a period of seven days on suspicion of IRA activity. Simmons' colleagues suspected he had informed on them during his detention. In May 1984, a man walking his dog near Dundalk discovered a skeleton in a bog which appeared to have a bullet wound to the skull. After forensic examination it was determined to be the remains of Simmons. In 1996, a Provo from the Castlewellan area, who had just been released from the H-Block, admitted to me that his unit had been responsible for the killing.

Even as recently as 1998, the bogs of Ireland were giving up their secrets. On 3 July, a body was discovered in a makeshift coffin in a shallow grave at Varna, Co. Galway where it is believed to have lain since the man's execution during the Irish Civil War. Contemporary reports show that Patrick Joyce, principal of Varna Boys National School, disappeared on 9 October 1920, after being tried and found guilty of treason. He was found fully clothed and with personal items such as a gold watch and a gold claddagh ring still on the body. The tools of his trade were contained in his pockets, namely a pen, a pencil and some chalk. A spent .22 round was also recovered from the grisly tomb.

The number of individuals who were missing would always cause debate. Remember, the only person that the Provos admitted to killing was Captain Nairac. They positively denied involvement in the others and went so far as to create fantastic stories to divert attention. The scandalous fiction surrounding Jean is well documented here, but even more amazing was the lengths to which they went in order to cover up their part in the murders of Bugsy and Bru. A female volunteer had visited the McKinney home a year or so after the lads had gone astray. She just thought as she was passing she might call to say she had met them both in Heathrow Airport, as they waited to board a flight ... to Mexico, she thought.

It wasn't long before the rumours took over and stories abounded about how successful the lads had been in their life as bank robbers. This effectively kept people, especially the families, from raising questions. If their sons were robbing banks, then they were unlikely to be broadcasting the fact. Locals, including Republicans, bragged about how their old mates were the Andersonstown version of Butch Cassidy and the Sundance Kid.

It appeared the Provisional IRA could disappear people at will and just let their propaganda department keep the families in the dark for years to come. Was it the uncertainty behind these individual killings that demanded the bodies be lost in a 'bog job' as opposed to being found on border roads?

From day one I wanted to be proved wrong about the number of missing people. Nothing would have pleased me more than to hear from someone we had believed murdered. Our constitution declared that we would:

> ... endeavour through public and political lobbying to secure the return of the remains of Northern Ireland's 'Disappeared'. To bury our loved ones with Christian dignity and to provide continued support for the grieving families.

The fact that, by now, the issue of 'the disappeared' was known around the globe made us proud. Against all the odds we had succeeded in getting our story out, regardless of threats.

Despite our best efforts and our wide coverage we had yet to uncover the whereabouts of even one of the bodies. More and more I was being approached by senior Provisionals who would go to great lengths to convince me that the issue had been at the top of their agenda and would, where 'possible', be resolved. They all, however, reiterated the fear of prosecutions. We had made things quite clear in this regard; to push for arrests would have been a nonsense, the procedures for the early release of prisoners was well under way and some of our group felt a trial would only serve to compound their agony. Granted, the court case might shed some light on the actual reason behind their loved one's disappearance, but then they would have to endure the release of the killers after a few months, if they were prosecuted at all. When I put this to Republicans they would reply: 'That's what you are saying now, but if a body is recovered, an inquest would follow and no doubt after hearing the gory details of the death, the families might wish to throw the book at the 'volunteers' involved.' They were right, and I knew it.

I recall that, about this time, Gerry Adams was asked a question by a reporter on the subject of 'Disappearance', to which he angrily replied: 'Disappeared is a good propaganda term, but these people are missing.' Of course he was right, the word was a good propaganda term, but it was purposely coined by me and not some agent in Whitehall, as he was implying. I knew that whatever title we chose, it would be more effective if it were linked to some similar atrocity that had happened or was happening elsewhere. The image I intended to conjure up was that of the barbaric way in which individuals had been disappeared in the South Americas by Governments hell bent on stopping democracy.

The word 'missing' that Gerry suggested, would have been more appropriate to describe a teenager who had quarrelled with his or her parents and run off, or a spouse who had done a bunk to start a new life. This is exactly what the Republican Movement wanted the world to think. They were 'Freedom Fighters' and so were totally opposed to disappearance as a form of warfare. I felt sure we would soon find the remains of one of the poor unfortunates we had come to represent, but I feared it would be by accident, rather than design. The whole issue held too much embarrassment for the Republican Movement to just come clean on their sordid history.

Every so often, especially after documentaries depicting our campaign, we would receive correspondence from the general public. These were usually letters of support and hope for the future, but also, more significantly, apologies from ex-Republicans for the actions of the organisation they once represented. I still have in my possession heart-breaking letters from old men who had, in their youth, fought gallantly against the 'Black and Tans' in the wars for independence; their shame at the actions of today's 'men of freedom' is palpable.

Instead of lobbying more politicians to secure support, (we believed we had succeeded with this) we changed our tactics and decided instead to write to individuals within the ranks of Republicanism, in the hope that they could add a fresh dimension. The response was truly surprising. Many told us that they would, or already had, raised the issue and firmly believed the IRA had no choice but to make known the locations of those that had been murdered and secretly buried. It would be a major setback but there was no alternative. They unanimously pointed to the fear of prosecutions and suggested I find someone to act as mediator, someone acceptable to both the IRA and ourselves. The difficulty for us was finding someone we could trust to be impartial. Many individuals and organisations offered their services, but we could not be sure they were, or could remain, objective.

For instance, we had been introduced to a trauma specialist, whose impressive CV showed that she had worked with victims all around the globe. When members of our group told me that during therapy sessions she seemed more interested in their sex lives than in their sorrow, I figured they had either misunderstood or were over-reacting. When these stories persisted, I began to wonder if we had a crank in our midst and started a little detective work of my own. I found out that the few people whose names she had volunteered as acquaintances, had either never heard of her or knew as little about her as I did.

Helen suspected that she was a spy. Who the spy was employed by was of more interest to me and I believe I came close to finding out when walking with her in Belfast city centre one day. This was just days before the visit of US President, Bill Clinton and the place was literally crawling with undercover agents. On turning a corner, I was absolutely amazed to hear about a dozen Special Branch men, who had just alighted from a Police wagon, call her by her first name. Obviously very embarrassed, she tried to explain them away by saying she knew them from duty work at a hospital where she had once been employed. Needless to say, her services were no longer required. Maybe I was reading too deeply into this encounter, but at least it illustrates how vulnerable, if not paranoid, we had become.

Fearing a repeat of our last experience of counselling, we decided it would be better to approach a statutory body which was properly regulated. We explained our situation and what the group members were enduring, to Victim Support, Northern Ireland. Although they expressed the deepest sympathy, they did nothing to alleviate the suffering. Even after thirty years of conflict I could only conclude that there was no one in Northern Ireland capable of counselling. Other groups who felt they had the necessary skills, showed interest in siding with our grief in order to put them in a better position to secure funding. These groups know only too well who they are and I only spare their names to protect victims who might have found them helpful in some way.

Periodically, certain journalists would attempt to coerce us into anti-Republican outbursts. When the 'Bloody Sunday' campaign appeared to be getting a lot of air time it would be suggested I release some statement or other to counteract them. Just where did these hacks think I was coming from? The campaign for the truth to be told about the butchery that went on in Derry was in no way in conflict with our own, in fact, it highlighted the murder of civilians which was exactly what we were doing. The only disparity was that these fourteen people were murdered by the British Army whereas Jean McConville was murdered by the 'People's army'. To add to that, I did not believe the 'Bloody Sunday' campaign was a Republican one at all.

When it came to relieving the suffering of a family though, we made no distinctions. I recall when the National Graves Association were pushing to have the body of hanged IRA man Tom Williams removed from Crumlin Road Prison so that he might be buried with his colleagues in the Republican plot at Milltown. As a group, we discussed the obvious similarities with our own predicaments and decided, at the risk of being accused of hijacking, to write to the then Secretary of State Patrick Mayhew, pleading with him to accede to the request, as we knew only too well how horrific it was to be denied a body for burial. My telephone was kept busy for the next couple of days as individuals, who strongly supported the Williams campaign, praised me for my support and for directing my input in a sensitive manner. A few of the 'dodgy hacks' reckoned I had missed a golden opportunity to kick the IRA in the teeth.

It is not easy to be a non-political force in Northern Ireland. No matter what you do or say, someone misinterprets and the simplest of statements can become an attack on something or other. 'I don't think Mr McKendry will help further his cause' or 'He should be more selective in his choice of bedfellow' were a couple of the comments that were never-ending. As far as I was concerned, the most basic of human rights was the right to life. It logically followed that it was a basic right to be prepared to meet your maker in a Christian fashion if you so wished.

If the war machine believed that our exile to rural Co. Down would be an effective form of censorship, they were to get a rude awakening. We were adamant that the campaign would become even more vocal.

On our return from a very welcome break in San Francisco, which was paid for by a very good (and very wealthy) American friend, we were brought down to earth with a sickening thud. The majority of our belongings, which had been 'secured' under tarpaulin as the cottage was too small, were distributed around the nearby fields. Storm force winds had paid a visit in our absence and we were left with waterlogged and uninsured belongings. This was truly a new beginning; new furniture, new clothes, new everything in fact. This was undoubtedly one of the lowest points of our entire existence.

Life had to go on though, and within days I was on the trail again. The Peace Train organisation had arranged for me to address the 'Forum for Peace and Reconciliation' in Dublin Castle. Knowing that all the political parties in the Republic would be present, I was actually looking forward to addressing them. As it happened, I was a nervous wreck, but felt I had said all that was needed. The bonus came when, like all the parties present, Sinn Féin, in the guise of Jim Gibney, proceeded to offer their sympathy for what the families had suffered. I thanked them, as I had all those present, but added that I doubted their sincerity and I had twenty-odd years of reasons for doing so.

A little while later, I was totally amazed to find ex-Taoiseach Albert Reynolds angrily pointing a finger at Mr Gibney, as he demanded they do something immediately to find a resolution. Was it my nervous stuttered speech that had moved this man, who would be considered by most to be pro-Nationalist, to become so vociferous? If it was, then I was indeed a happy man. More and more it became clear that the Republican Movement were being isolated on 'the disappeared' issue. Not a day went past that we weren't praised in some way for our stance and, more and more, it was Republicans that were lauding the praise.

The initial hope of the Provos that our campaign would blow over was fast fading. They really had to take stock now and figure out how best to hold their heads up whilst being criticised by all and sundry. The sky-blue campaign ribbon that we had adopted was appearing in the strangest of places. I had even seen people wear both it and the Saoirse ribbon on the same lapel. I had no trouble with this as I believed the early release of political prisoners (which the green Saoirse emblem represented) was an essential part of the normalisation process. Many of my pals had found themselves behind bars for what they believed in, and I can say categorically that the same lads would never have received so much as a parking ticket in a normal society.

BREAKING THROUGH

Helen had just beaten me to the telephone and as I watched her I knew there was something amiss. The caller was male and claimed he had been compelled to ring after watching a television plea from myself just recently.

He was apologising and went on to admit that he had been a member of the team that had snatched Jean from her home in 1972. He told how he and a colleague had hijacked a van from Clonard Street on the Falls and, as directed, drove to Divis Flats picking up several members of 'Cumann na mBan' en route. They were to arrest both Jean and a neighbour, but finding only Jean at home, they took the panic-stricken woman to a house in Beechmount Grove where she was handed over to an intelligence unit. He once again stated how sorry he was for his involvement in the affair, but that it was only recently he realised the poor woman had never been returned to her family.

We were flabbergasted. The vehicle he claimed to have used tallied with the one Archie had described at the time his mother was taken away. What gave us more hope was the address he had taken her to; it was the same as that given by those who had spoken to the priest some time back. The caller went on to claim that he had been trying to pass on what he knew for weeks now, and had in fact left a message on the freephone line that had been set up by Women and Victims Empowered (WAVE), a stress and trauma group. When we later queried this group about the man's claim, they suggested the message had been erased accidentally. Perhaps so, but why did they not bother to tell us about the call? Once again, other groups were complicating things rather than helping.

Whether this information was fabricated or not, that house in Beechmount took on some kind of eerie attraction for us. Often we would drive up there to check out what remained of its garden. I even asked the RUC if they would consider sending in a forensic team to look for hair or blood traces that might indicate whether or not Jean had been there. They felt such a search would be a waste of time considering the period of time that had lapsed since. In hindsight, considering the cease-fire had just broken I couldn't really blame them. After all, the whole story could have been concocted, and might simply have been a ruse to lure a crowd of policemen to their deaths, this was also the principal reason why I didn't try to enter the derelict building.

The morning news told the chilling tale of the discovery of what appeared to be human remains in the Derriaghy area, just outside Belfast.

I immediately called the RUC as I had done on numerous occasions when similar finds had been made. 'Could the body possibly be that of Jean McConville?', I asked. 'Absolutely not', I was assured. Although the remains were of a female between the ages of twenty and forty, they could say quite confidently that they weren't there long enough to be Jean's. We breathed a sigh of relief and talked for hours about the heartache that someone somewhere must be enduring.

Around 10 p.m. that evening, there was a phone call for Helen. The RUC inspector asked if she could describe what her mother had been wearing the day she disappeared. Ashen-faced, she described in minute detail the clothing her mum had worn, even giving precise details as to the make up of the very buttons on a cardigan. In a short space of time (that seemed an eternity) we would be called to be told, once again, that the remains could not possibly be Jean's as the unfortunate victim had never had children. How could a professional force make such a hash of things? There were no apologies either for frightening Helen half to death. Two years later the 'young female' remains were identified as a young man aged twenty-three from Antrim town.

Being an avid reader on forensic science since childhood, I figured the only way to be sure such a cock-up would never be repeated was to ask the RUC to establish a DNA base, which would permit the speedy identification of remains in the future. This was shortly afterwards implemented when members of all the families of the disappeared went along to their local police stations to give a blood sample.

One very sad aspect of things, was the amount of calls I was beginning to receive from families who had had a son, husband, wife or daughter disappear for no apparent reason. In heart-breaking voices they would explain how their loved-one had just up and left. I am sure the grief they endured was no different to our own. There were organisations out there which specialised in reuniting people in these situations and all I could do was offer my sympathies and direct them towards the specialists.

We continued to demand that Sinn Féin put more pressure on their military wing to do something soon to allow us to bury our dead in a Christian manner. Most of the parents were pensioners by now and we hoped they would have the opportunity to give their sons a dignified burial, before they died themselves. After a flurry of media attention which demanded that Adams meet with us to clarify Sinn Féin's position, we were pleasantly surprised to receive an invite to attend Connolly House. The meeting began with the usual rhetoric about how terrible war was and how glad they were that things like that no longer happened.

'There is no doubt, the IRA killed your mother.' These were the words with which Gerry Adams, for the first time, admitted what had happened. He went on to warn us of the perils and pitfalls of having dealings with the Press. He said he now realised it was an issue that had to be resolved. Afterwards, we discussed his change of mind, still unsure of his commitment to actually do something. At least now there were no denials of involvement.

Not long after our meeting with Adams, every telephone conversation we had pointed to the imminent arrival of news in the form of a statement from the IRA. One 'well-placed' journalist told us that the IRA were on the brink of releasing details of a 'Special Unit' dedicated solely to discovering the whereabouts of 'the disappeared'. Others were adamant that only details of those that the IRA had killed in error would be made known. We only half believed what we were being told; how could you hide your involvement in something so horrific for so many years and just all of a sudden turn around and accept blame?

Just a week or so after our meeting with Adams in Connolly House, I received a call from a friend in the newspaper business asking if I could be in a city centre bar the next day for a lunchtime pint. I could tell there was more to it than that, but decided to go anyway.

For half an hour I stood on my own at the bar. I could see my friend at the rear of the place in deep conversation with someone whose face was vaguely familiar to me. Eventually, I was called over and introduced to Gino Gallagher, the then Officer Commanding of the INLA, an organisation which was almost extinct due to bitter in-fighting. I was remotely chuffed when he declared he needed no introduction, he had known who I was when I first entered the pub.

Gallagher went on to say that he was amazed to find that I was still alive, after 'the knocking' I had given the Provos. If I had concentrated my efforts on the INLA, they would have had no hesitation in silencing me at an early stage, before I got started. In his next breath, he was praising me for the stance I had taken, and better again said that he thought Helen had 'more balls than the whole road put together'.

It was inevitable that the conversation would come round to discussing Seamus Ruddy from Newry. He didn't know an awful lot about the Ruddy affair but before I left he had promised that a statement would be released to the Press. In it they would state that they had killed Ruddy and would be doing everything in their power to allow his family to recover the body, which he suggested was somewhere outside Paris. He quite liked my suggestion about stealing a march on the Provos. The INLA had always attracted a bad Press and a bit of compassion like this would surely allow them to be seen in a better light.

Just two weeks later, at the Social Security Office on the Falls Road, Gallagher died in a hail of bullets, his so-called comrades bullets I might add. True to his word though, he had said his piece to the *Irish News* in the days after our meeting and thankfully before his bloody demise. He admitted that Ruddy had been murdered and promised that the party would use its influence to locate the body and return it to the Ruddy family.

We soon realised that we had no one to depend on for support. The parents of the others who had been taken were elderly or in some cases dead. I didn't expect camera-shy old ladies to walk the streets of our cities with placards. Standing freezing cold outside public buildings, with only our children and a few good friends to support us, often made us think about how easy it would be to pack it all in.

These vigils were absolutely essential we felt, as they brought the issue to the general public. As miserable as it was to stand all day in the snow and rain, someone always managed to brighten our day. We would have Jewish people who had survived the Holocaust and could never understand the inhumanity of man, or guys who had recently been released from the 'blocks' and now wanted to give solace to people who had suffered as a result of their past actions. The latter comments always bolstered us because we knew these past combatants also told the Republican Movement the same.

Were the rumours about the Provos setting up a Special Unit to find the remains true? It looked that way when, at Christmas time in 1998, the RUC announced that they had begun excavating at Glen Colin Housing Estate in Andersonstown, for the bodies of John McClory and Brian McKinney. They announced that the dig was in response to an anonymous tip off that had been received yet again at the WAVE office. Was this credible? After all, information had come forward over the years suggesting the boys were indeed buried here. Why all of a sudden were they prepared to act on a tip off?

Something was definitely amiss but I couldn't quite put my finger on it. The two families were forced to watch while the Police search teams, using the latest echo-sounding equipment from France, dug up the pathways of the estate. When asked to speak on the radio and television about the dig, I found it very difficult to respond, even though I still believed the lads were somewhere on the estate. To begin with, the excavation was happening a few hundred yards from a spot which the CI5 (murder squad) and I had agreed to be the most likely burial place. We had made this decision based on the information we had gleaned since our inquiries began. Also, they had always insisted they could not take action on hearsay alone. As it happened, the dig proved to be fruitless, and the families were left to wonder if they would ever retrieve their sons.

I requested a meeting with the detectives in charge shortly afterwards and was nothing short of bewildered when they admitted that the dig had been 'a very successful publicity exercise'. They went on to tell me about the amount of media

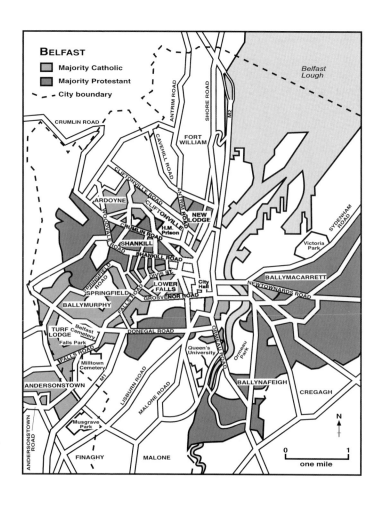

BELFAST

- ▨ Majority Catholic
- ▨ Majority Protestant
- ⌐ ⌐ City boundary

Belfast Lough

CRUMLIN ROAD

ANTRIM ROAD

SHORE ROAD

M2

CAVEHILL ROAD

FORT WILLIAM

CLIFTONVILLE ROAD

ARDOYNE

ANTRIM ROAD

CLIFTONVILLE

NEW LODGE

WOODVALE ROAD

CRUMLIN ROAD

H.M. Prison

SHANKILL

SHANKILL ROAD

DIVIS ST.

LOWER FALLS

City Hall

BALLYMACARRETT

SYDENHAM ROAD

Victoria Park

NEWTOWNARDS ROAD

SPRINGFIELD ROAD

SPRINGFIELD

GROSVENOR ROAD

BALLYMURPHY

FALLS ROAD

DONEGAL ROAD

TURF LODGE

Belfast Cemetery

Falls Park

Queen's University

ORMEAU ROAD

Ormeau Park

Milltown Cemetery

FALLS ROAD

M1

LISBURN ROAD

MALONE ROAD

BALLYNAFEIGH

CREGAGH

ANDERSONSTOWN

ANDERSONSTOWN ROAD

Musgrave Park

FINAGHY

MALONE

N

0   1

one mile

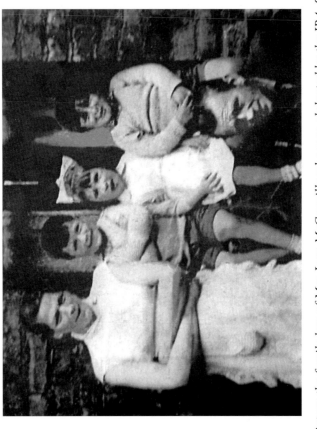

The only picture the family has of Mrs Jean McConville who was abducted by the IRA. She is seen here with her children Robert, Helen, Arthur (Junior) and her husband Arthur (bottom right).

Séamus and Helen were married in 1976 at the tender age of eighteen.

Helen McKendry (née McConville) and her husband Séamus stand outside Belfast City Hall seeking signatures for the Families of the Disappeared campaign.

The Families of the Disappeared campaign is officially launched in the Linenhall Library in Belfast in June 1995.

A service was conducted in St Patrick's Cathedral, Armagh to remember those who have disappeared during the troubles and to show support for their families.

The remains of Eamon Molloy from North Belfast are left in a recently purchased coffin in a corner of Faughart Cemetery, just north of Dundalk, in May 1999.

In 1998, the RUC began excavating at Glen Road in Andersonstown, for the bodies of John McClory and Brian McKinney.

John McClory and Brian McKinney (Bru and Bugsy as they where known to everyone), joined the list of the disappeared in 1978.

Gerry Evans, aged twenty-four, from Rathview Park, Cross-maglen, described as a family lad, was last seen on 27 March 1979.

Charlie Armstrong with his grandson Adrian in the last picture taken before his disappearance on 16 August 1991.

Mrs Anne Morgan, sister of Seamus Ruddy, reads out a statement on behalf of the family following a confrontation with IRSP leadership in Belfast in 1985.

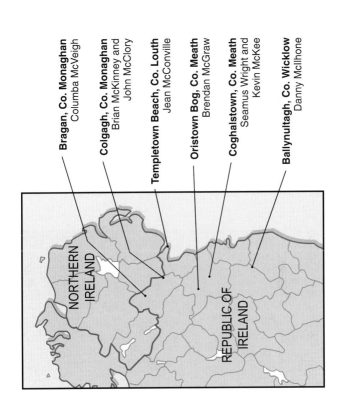

Bragan, Co. Monaghan
Columba McVeigh

Colgagh, Co. Monaghan
Brian McKinney and
John McClory

Templetown Beach, Co. Louth
Jean McConville

Oristown Bog, Co. Meath
Brendan McGraw

Coghalstown, Co. Meath
Seamus Wright and
Kevin McKee

Ballynultagh, Co. Wicklow
Danny McIlhone

NORTHERN
IRELAND

REPUBLIC OF
IRELAND

The burial sites given by the IRA in their statement in March 1999.

In June 1999, after four weeks of excavation in the bog at Colgagh, the remains of John McClory and Brian McKinney were found.

John McClory's mother kisses her son's coffin after finally bringing him home.

Around 70 locals gather for a service and to offer help and support at the dig for the remains of Jean McConville in Carlingford, Co. Louth.

Gardaí painstakingly dig for evidence at Carlingford showing a skill second to none in skimming off just a couple of inches of earth at a time in order to protect possible evidence.

As the country basked in the heat of the hottest day for three years, in July 1999, Séamus and Helen McKendry were still 'camped out' after five weeks of the dig. Three diggers were being used by the Gardai and the rolling sea mists often obscured the ends of the search site.

The strain is starting to show on Séamus and Helen McKendry as they watch and wait at the dig for Helen's mother's remains at Carlingford.

The IRA pinpointed a spot beneath the car park at Templetown beach as the burial place of Jean McConville.

Only the remains of flowers left by sympathisers lie scattered on the excavation site where, after seven weeks, the Gardaí ceased digging.

Helen sits in front of the shrine erected by Séamus McKendry to remember Jean McConville on the beach at Carlingford.

coverage the digs had generated and I believe they honestly thought they had furthered our cause somehow. As far as I was concerned, the only thing generated was grief and sleepless nights for the two families directly affected and something similar for the remainder of us on the periphery of events.

You would think that we would have been used to this sort of crap, but we weren't and it made us begin to regret ever having started the whole affair. Much as I hate to admit it, my back problem was getting worse and I wanted nothing more than to walk or should I say stumble to more peaceful pasture. Believe me, there was nothing I desired more than a day off from it all. Gone were the days of seeing the campaign as a panacea, it was now threatening my sanity.

One person whom I have neglected to mention, indeed honour in all of this is a man named John Manley. He came on board with Helen and I, not to become embroiled in campaigning, but rather to enhance his degree studies at the University of Jordanstown. John had a knack of dealing with our difficulties to which no one else could come close. His irritating mid-Atlantic accent drove me to despair, yet his naïveté was heart-warming. John was one of life's nicer people and I truly regret putting him in some of the predicaments we encountered.

I recall the pair of us at the Glencree Summer workshop, a forum on human rights abuse in Co. Wicklow, and how he had tried to defuse the imminent confrontation between myself and Sinn Féin the next day. The next morning I could feel his embarrassment as I launched into a stuttered version of the Convention on Human Rights, at least that was what I intended. Instead it came out as a tirade of abuse directed towards the Sinn Féin delegation present. What saved my skin on this occasion, was the inadequacy of the Republican team, Conor Murphy and his sidekick. Flabbergasted at my presence and the abuse I was hurling, they made the unforgivable decision to turn their backs on me. This didn't, of course, go unnoticed by the very many enlightened people who were in attendance and scrutinising from the floor. The 'Shinners' left quite abruptly that day, unable to justify their presence at a forum on human rights abuse.

Primarily in our own interests, and in an attempt to placate them, we once again rang the 'Shinners' to enquire about the prospects of a meeting. Their agreement took us quite by surprise. Were we been taken seriously, or were the coffee and doughnuts available to all? I subsequently saw this as a turning point. Helen and I were being treated as real people with real concerns. Gerry Adams started the discourse by telling us the IRA had undoubtedly killed Jean. Although he had admitted this before, it was good to have it reiterated at this time.

We knew we had the Republican Movement where we wanted them. For all the years of lying, all the scandalous twisted rumours, they were now forced to back-pedal. He claimed a huge effort was being undertaken to discover the reason behind Jean's abduction and I actually believed him. The relief on Helen's face spoke volumes, at least the stigma of having a mother who resided with soldiers or Loyalists could be eradicated from her life once and for all.

If we thought Adams was going to make things easier for us then we were soon reminded differently. Once again, he attempted to justify his side of things by saying that terrible things had happened since 1969, perpetrated by all the factions. When he began the rhetoric I interjected and said, 'look, you are hell-bent on distancing yourself from IRA activity so why are we even talking to you, tell the IRA we want to meet with them face to face, they can even wear their balaclavas if they so desire'. Lapsing into deep thought, he finally said that he felt my suggestion to be a good one and would pass on my request to certain people. Before leaving that day he confided to me that we had succeeded in getting the support of 'ninety-nine per cent of the Republican Movement behind our endeavours'. I remarked that this was quite a change in Republican thought from just two short years ago. Our mood was distinctly upbeat as we drove across the city to Stormont for a meeting with Security Minister Adam Ingram.

We were aware of some million pounds or so in the Victim's Committee coffers and we were going to Stormont to enquire if we might avail of some money to purchase a decent computer to enable us to set up a website. I was nothing short of gobsmacked when Ingram declared that he could not duplicate resources. 'How can you duplicate zero?', I angrily commented. We had never had a penny from the Victim's Fund or any other for that matter. It became clear that in their wisdom the 'suits' at Stormont had funded the WAVE group for their work on 'the disappeared' issue.

What work? How many encounters had they had with the Provisionals or Sinn Féin? How much of their personal savings had they pumped into campaigning over the years? We were totally and utterly disgusted and refused to grovel anymore. We had quite simply been hijacked and were powerless to do anything about it. That was it, never again would we lower ourselves to beg for scraps.

Maybe if the IRA, the INLA or the LVF were to publicise the fact that they were actively doing something to alleviate the suffering of relatives of those they had murdered, then they too could claim funding. I felt sick in my stomach, and not for the first time seriously thought about jacking the whole thing in.

In my heart I knew I never would, my promise to Helen all those years ago would reverberate in my mind and I would find myself once again putting pen to paper and concentrating my anger on those directly responsible for the murders and subsequent anguish.

Our anger abated that evening when we received a call from Maol Muire Tynan of *The Irish Times*, a woman credited with being knowledgeable in Republican thought. She told us that an IRA statement was imminent and that they had, as we were led to believe, set up a Special Unit to ascertain where 'the disappeared' were located. If it were true, this was great news. I wondered how I could have even considered walking away when our small group had forced the Provisional IRA to capitulate and confess to its horrific deeds.

It seemed that Tynan had indeed done her homework for I met 'the queer fella' the next day and he was able to say that not only had a Special Unit been created, but it consisted of their top brass. This was more than I could have wished for, it showed how seriously the IRA were about resolving the issue. We were assured that the question was always to the fore when Government representatives and Republicans met. Political parties also assured us that they raised the matter at every possible opportunity, by now the Provos must have been sick to the teeth of the name Jean McConville, not to mention her daughter and myself.

If the IRA were as supportive as Adams suggested, then I wish they had told their foot soldiers because the abuse and threats continued. One imbecile even offered to challenge me on national television about my claim that Jean had been murdered. I welcomed the challenge, but heard no more of it. I can only surmise that his colleagues gave him a bollocking, for on our next meeting his words were inaudible and he could only offer a glare.

Four weeks after our meeting with Adams, we received a phone call from a Sinn Féin member who said that the IRA had consented to a meeting, but would see only Helen.

The cowardly bastards wouldn't face me, but they were prepared to invite Jean McConville's daughter into their lair. Helen did not like the thought of emulating her mother's demise and we both felt that the IRA were hoping that she would be too afraid to attend. Very courageously and against my advice, she accepted the terms being offered. All I could do was make sure someone else knew of the planned meeting and so I phoned a few journalists and explained the proposed itinerary.

On 22 October 1997 (my fortieth birthday), we nervously set off for Connolly House in Andersonstown. The entire journey was taken up with my warning Helen of where not to go and what not to say. I don't really know who was worrying the most. On our arrival, we witnessed a scene that was like something from a keystone cop movie: the road was black with policemen and jeeps, worse again a helicopter hovered above the building. I felt sure the meeting would be cancelled as the IRA would think we had alerted the Police. Although we hadn't called the Police and didn't know who did, I felt somewhat reassured by their presence. My plan to make sure Helen was always in my line of vision fell asunder when a rented mob appeared and in the melee I lost sight of her. The next hour was probably the longest of my life as I scrambled around the streets hoping to catch a glimpse of her.

I was on the verge of going up to one of the RUC vehicles when Helen, still shaking, got back into the car. Her account of events would have to wait, all I wanted to do was get the hell out of the area. It took a couple of stiff whiskeys to steady her nerves (and mine) before she was capable of telling me what had happened. Using the crowd as cover, they had slipped her out a side entrance to a waiting car and then driven round local streets in a bid to confuse her. This was pointless really as she knew the area exceptionally well. Dropped off in Lenadoon Avenue, just a mile away, she was directed to enter an apartment, where a group of unmasked (thankfully) men offered her a seat and choice of beverages. They were every bit as nervous as her, and didn't try to conceal it. 'Wouldn't it look great if the cops kicked the door in?', they humoured and asked if Helen and I had notified the Police of our movements.

'The IRA killed your mother, that is, the old IRA of the seventies, and not today's well-organised fighting force.' They went on to tell Helen that they were the unit tasked with discovering the fate of those who had gone 'missing'. To be successful, they needed to have all the information available. Helen gave the details of those she knew to have been part of the abduction party and other information they requested. They treated her with respect and apologised for the actions of their comrades, but when asked if they would publicly do so, they declined to comment. Given a fiver, she was directed to a waiting taxi and wished well for the future.

I was very much intrigued by their admission, but more so when I discovered just how senior those in the IRA squad were. I contacted a few newspaper pals and soon accumulated an extensive gallery of known Provos. When Helen immediately pointed to the Chief of Staff of the IRA, I felt sure she must have been mistaken. She was adamant, however, that this was the man who had been in charge of proceedings. His Chief Assistant was also very well known to us (and undoubtedly every cop in Ireland) as a major player in three decades of war games. The third senior member of the team was very well known by myself; he was out on early release from Long Kesh prison.

This was nothing short of incredible, the IRA command was not allowing junior members to investigate the disappearances but were actually assigning themselves the task. I was becoming the thorn that I had promised to be in the sides of the Provos. Why else would they be taking things so seriously? The Clinton Administration were assuring us that they were continuing to raise the topic when they spoke with Sinn Féin. The Brits and the Southern Government were doing likewise and, more importantly, every Republican with a shred of conscience was kicking up a stink over the whole affair.

SMALL VICTORIES

Every so often we heard from Helen's brothers. Relations had been souring for years and they had become known to us as the 'brothers grim', simply because when we did receive a call, it would invariably cause us upset. They were never happy with anything Helen or I did, yet it never struck them to actually help us. They always claimed to have spoken 'to the right people', those that 'knew the proper way of things'. This always infuriated me: the IRA command had just met with Helen to discuss and hopefully resolve matters, yet the word of some idiot they had met in a pub would be gospel to them.

We reverted back to the waiting, something we were only too used to doing. It never got any easier, there were so many crests and troughs that you never really knew if you were winning or losing. This mental torture was played through until Christmas 1998, when we finally received some news. Fr Pat McCafferty, a young priest who had volunteered to assist us when necessary, rang to say he had had a visit from Gerry Adams and that things would be resolved very soon. Adams would be saying something of importance in his New Year message. Although eager to believe, we had heard things like this before and didn't allow it to lead to complacency. I often thought that the Provos must have expected that by giving us a hint of imminent happenings, we would shut up and allow them some extra time. This amounted to censorship and I was having none of it.

Almost straight away I put a demand in the papers that the IRA issue a statement that would effectively give amnesty to its own members (both past and present) who gave information about the disappearances. After all, if the organisation was genuine about resolving matters, then this would guarantee the passage of much needed data while providing a safety clause for the 'volunteers'.

To further this, I contacted the BBC and was delighted when they agreed to give me some air time on the main news, though they doubted if they could get a Sinn Féin representative to join me on the piece. At the last minute, however, I was informed that Mitchell McLaughlin, the then Sinn Féin Party Chairman from Derry, had consented to appear. I had met Mitchell a year or two previously whilst attending a Labour Party Conference in Brighton and had found him apparently sympathetic to my demands. As it happened, I didn't get the support I had naïvely expected. When asked to join me in a call for IRA members or ex-members to be given a guarantee of safety, he declined, and reverted to the party line that Sinn Féin was doing all in its power to relieve the injustice put on the suffering families. Was any member of the Sinn Féin organisation permitted to voice their personal opinion on matters? I doubted it.

We were soon to be visited by a couple of priests from Clonard Monastery in Belfast, Fr Alex and Fr Brendan. Fr Alex Reid, the better known to us of the two, told us that he had been given the position of intermediary between the Provos and the families. Alex and Brendan soon became regular callers at our home.

They expressed their belief that the IRA were indeed genuine about a speedy resolution but were deeply concerned about the possibility of arrests and prosecutions. From day one we had made it patently clear that this was not what was important to us. Once again my cryptic side took over: why would the IRA be overly concerned by arrests? To begin with, they were all trained in anti-interrogation techniques and had been regular 'guests' at the likes of Castlereagh and Gough Barracks and were quite adept at withholding information. Quite apart from this, they knew fine well that even if convicted they would, under the existing early release of prisoners scheme, walk away in a relatively short space of time.

The priests spoke of a possible amnesty. Not the type I had envisaged where the IRA would offer one to its volunteers, but a general amnesty, agreed by both the British and Irish Governments. This would, they inferred, give a clear way for the individuals who had been closest to the barbarity of the early days of the conflict to come forward with the details necessary to bring events to a close. Our opinion on the suggested amnesty was sought and we voiced our unchanging belief that prosecutions would be farcical. All we wanted was to be able to bury our dead in consecrated grounds. I have never possessed much in the line of Christian thought (much to my dear mother's concern) but I really believe that even a dog deserves to be buried with dignity. The priests agreed to convey our thoughts to the IRA and both Governments.

I had always considered Fr Alex Reid to be a staunch Republican supporter and I had no opinion on his pastoral colleague. I must admit, both Helen and I had serious reservations about their part in events. When they asserted that, when bodies were recovered, the ensuing funerals should be low-key affairs, so as to keep the Media at bay, we quickly disagreed. Both Helen and I said that we wanted every television crew to know that they would be extremely welcome. We wanted the world to know just how barbaric war really was, even the type carried out by oppressed peoples. I never allowed myself to be censored by anyone and I wasn't about to let an organisation like Sinn Féin change that, particularly since they themselves had been the victims of censorship for far too long.

Speaking of media interest, it wasn't very long before we had another in the ever-growing list of documentary companies demanding the right to do a piece. This time it was a London outfit, October Films. From the outset, I told their representative of our reluctance to participate. To begin with, we had had our fill of crews taking over our lives. Going without food at our regular times was getting beyond a joke. It was bad enough for Helen and myself, but at least we would usually be taken to some fancy restaurant or other at the end of filming, our children weren't.

The TV companies chose restaurants where they themselves could be 'seen'. Being 'seen' meant nothing to us and we only considered that it was a shame to spend so much on the paltry servings of unpronounceable offerings when giving us the money would have stocked our larder for a week. We had already sworn that we were not going to entertain any more crews: the campaign had already ensured that the world knew about the *Families of the Disappeared*. October Films sent over their résumé and, like a fool, I was sucked in by some of their recent pieces, particularly the work they had done to highlight the plight of different Soviet minorities.

On arrival, the crew diverted almost immediately from the proposed script. They had claimed the piece would be a sympathetic insight into what Helen and I had been forced to endure since beginning our quest for the truth. Within minutes they were looking for phone numbers for the 'brothers grim', which were 'essential to the making of the documentary', they claimed. We couldn't quite understand this and feared their inclusion would only create strife. They had never been in the slightest bit interested in our affairs and to be honest their recollection of events from 1972 left a lot to be desired. The truth was, the Channel 4 team had arrived at a time when we were totally preoccupied with waiting by the telephone for news about the threatened IRA statement on the bodies. We had nobody to blame but ourselves for their presence; some day I would be brash enough to say 'No!' and mean it. October Films might have messed up on the script, but their sense of timing was impeccable; on 29 March 1999 the Republican leadership issued the statement we had long been promised.

In the lengthy statement, the IRA leadership apologised and accepted responsibility for the 'injustice of prolonging the suffering of victim's families by burying the bodies secretly'. They went on to claim that the bodies were located after an eighteen-month investigation by a Special Unit under the command of one of its most senior officers. They were admitting to the secret burial of ten people, but claimed that after a dozen or so attempts, they had been unsuccessful in tracing the remains of Captain Robert Nairac, the undercover British soldier who vanished in 1978.

They were careful not to give the exact whereabouts of any bodies until legislation, which we learned was imminent, effectively protected them from prosecutions. Our joy at their admittance to Jean's murder was short-lived when they went on to say that 'she had been arrested by Óglaigh na hÉireann in 1972 and had admitted to being an army spy'. Helen cried as she read aloud the affront to her mother's memory and I fought hard to stop myself from joining her. I forced myself into believing I had been prepared for more scurrilous allegations, but it still hurt a lot.

I tried to comfort Helen by telling her that no one believed that her mother had been guilty of any offence, not even the bastards who killed her or the Provo chiefs. Her only 'crime' was to be brought up a Protestant. This was nothing more than a sop to their moronic followers who needed a reason to excuse gestapo-style warfare.

The reasons behind the deaths of the others were equally pathetic. Seamus Wright from Belfast 'was court martialled in 1972 and found guilty of being a British agent and member of The Military Reaction Force', an undercover army operation believed to be responsible for many sectarian murders in the early seventies. They went on to claim that his fellow 'volunteer', Kevin McKee, was executed for the same reasons. Seventeen-year-old Columba McVeigh from Co. Tyrone was shot dead after admitting to being 'directed by the British Army to infiltrate Óglaigh na hÉireann'. Brendan Megraw from Belfast, was executed in 1978 after admitting to accusations of being an 'agent provocateur'. The killings of John McClory and Brian McKinney in 1978 and the 1981 murder of Danny McIlhone were justified by claiming they had 'used Provo weapons for personal gain'. So it was okay for this organisation, that was forever screaming about the abuses in the British judicial system, to carry out summary execution. There was no opportunity for defence for the victims; just an accusation, a barbaric period of torture and a bullet in the back of the head. Once again Republican hypocrisy at its best.

One name I hadn't really expected to see on the death list was Brendan Megraw from Twinbrook in Belfast. I had been convinced that his disappearance was at the hands of Military Intelligence. An even bigger surprise was their admittance to being responsible for killing an Eamon Molloy from North Belfast in 1975. Their claim that he was one of their members and that he had informed on them really shocked us all. We had never heard of Molloy and were totally confused as to why they would admit to a death that was not in our files. I received call after call from frantic journalists wanting to know something about him, but I was as confused as they were.

The statement that accompanied the list read:

> Eighteen months ago we established a special unit under the command of one of our most senior officers to ascertain the whereabouts of a number of people executed and buried by Óglaigh na hÉireann approximately twenty years ago.

These burials took place prior to an Army Council directive that the body of anyone killed by Óglaigh na hÉireann should be left for burial by their relatives. This issue has caused incalculable pain and distress to a number of families over a period of many years.

Despite many complicating factors which have both hampered and protracted this investigation, including the lapse in time, changes in leadership and the deaths of both members and former members of Óglaigh na hÉireann who were involved, we can now conclude this inquiry.

We believe we have established the whereabouts of the graves of nine people, some of whom were members of Óglaigh na hÉireann who were executed for activities which put other Óglaigh na hÉireann personnel at risk or jeopardised the struggle. Information regarding the location of these graves is now being processed and will hopefully result in the speedy retrieval of the bodies.

As we have previously stated, we are not responsible for all those previously listed in the media as having gone missing over the last thirty years. We are responsible for those we have acknowledged today and their families have all been notified.

In initiating this investigation our intention has been to do all within our power to rectify an injustice for which we accept full responsibility and to alleviate the suffering of the families. We are sorry that this has taken so long to resolve and for the prolonged anguish caused to the families.

My thoughts that night were not for the families of those named in the statement, but instead for those who had been omitted, such as the Armstrong and Evans families from Crossmaglen whose loved-ones were now even more 'disappeared' than ever before. I could only imagine their hopelessness that night as the flawed list of victims was read out. I felt that we were being used in a cynical fashion, as pawns in the bigger political game.

The general response to the heartless statement was nothing we hadn't expected. The mothers of John McClory and Brian McKinney described the news as 'great'. Taoiseach Bertie Ahern 'hoped it would have a positive impact on the Peace Process' and Gerry Adams, of course, welcomed the statement adding that his position after being contacted some years ago by the families was that:

> ... if any Republican organisation had killed members of those families, and the families were denied the right to bury their loved ones, then that was an injustice that should be rectified. If today's news means that is going to be the case, then Sinn Féin clearly welcomes that — it is a wrong that has been righted.

In an obvious reference to my cynical comments regarding the timing of the statement, a senior British official denied the development was an attempt to soften the Unionist position and remarked that 'it is not something we regard as a bargaining chip'.

Apart from the issue of decommissioning, we were the only other stumbling block to the Republican Movement being accepted as worthy of a place in the new assembly of Northern Ireland. It was therefore in their immediate interest to be seen to move on the matter of 'the disappeared'.

A further visit from Fr Alex Reid confirmed that legislation had been drafted for both Westminster and the Dáil which would in effect give the killers immunity from prosecutions in both jurisdictions.

Meanwhile, October Films had proceeded to set up a meeting of the McConville family despite our reservations. A Belfast hotel was chosen and Helen tried to explain to the crew, once again, that she believed it would be a waste of time;

hers was a family in name only and they just weren't capable of pulling together for any purpose. In front of the cameras, they behaved in a somewhat civil fashion (the verbal abuse was kept to a minimum at least) and even consented to Helen's choice of funeral; she wanted to welcome the 'media circus' that would inevitably arrive. Some of the brothers had expressed their desire to take their mother's body to Twinbrook for a wake, but Helen and Mickey both opposed this as Archie's wife had said some very cruel things about Jean in the past and offered 'alternate' reasons for her disappearance. In the end, it was reluctantly agreed that Helen, as the only family member who had fought to discover the truth, should be the one to determine how things would be conducted. Unfortunately, this agreement would be short-lived.

On 27 May 1999, The Northern Ireland Location of Victim's Remains Bill was presented in the House of Commons. It was, according to Secretary of State Mo Mowlam, 'entirely designed to relieve years of suffering' and was a limited amnesty primarily concerned with identifying the sites where people were buried. The Unionists and quite a few Conservatives opposed the bill. Gerry Fitt angered me when he drew unwarranted comparisons with the Paratroopers who had murdered fourteen civilians in Derry in 1972. He called for immunity for them too. Perhaps what is good for one side is good for the other, but he was using us to further his own agenda and in this way he was no different to Sinn Féin. I had never forgiven Fitt for his bungling input in 1973, when I believe he helped the Provos dispose of Jean McConville by calling for the Press to back off.

I had been sent a copy of the legislation a few days earlier and had been unable to fully understand the worth of it as it was written in typical legalese. Neither Helen nor any of the other relatives were happy at the thought of the killers being exculpated, but their hands were tied. The most important thing to them was bringing their loved ones home for a respectable burial.

A welcome attempt at amending the Bill came from the Liberal Democrat's spokesperson on Northern Ireland affairs, Leonid Opik MP. His first amendment called for the Secretary of State to pay for the cost of the funerals, should the ensuing digs be successful. Secondly, he proposed that families of those whose remains are located, should be eligible for compensation 'under existing schemes'. This referred to the compensation entitlement for victims of paramilitary violence, but if a claim for compensation is not made within three years of the victim's demise then it is null and void. I have promised that my next drive, after the recovery of the bodies, will be to go to the European Courts, if necessary, to overturn this absurd ruling. In Helen's case, for example, her mother had previously been recognised only as a 'missing person' and not as a victim. There has recently been a suggestion that a sum of £10,000 be paid to those families who were bereaved as a result of the conflict, including those known as 'the disappeared'.

The Bill was passed in the Commons by an overwhelming 324 votes to ten. The MPs had, I am glad to say, put their revulsion at the amnesty behind them and compassionately voted to help us reach a speedy resolution. The Lords refused to give it such an easy passage, but it still went through. It was also accepted by both the Dáil and the Seanad.

The International Commission set up to oversee the retrieval of the victims was to be headed by Sir Kenneth Bloomfield, former head of the Civil Service in Northern Ireland, and ex-Tánaiste John Wilson.

The waiting was nothing short of cruel. Sleep was impossible and even holding food down became a struggle. Having the documentary team living on top of us did little to ease the strain.

At 7:15 a.m. on Friday 28 May 1999 we were woken from our light sleep by a call from a local radio presenter who astonished us by saying a body had been found just south of the border and suggesting that it could be Jean's. The emotional discharge was intense and neither of us could talk or think straight. Soon after, a friend from RTE rang to say that the body was male and definitely on the list of the nine that the Provos had admitted killing.

Rather than saddened by the fact that it couldn't be her mother, Helen expressed delight that someone, somewhere was going to have peace of mind that day. I found this unbelievably unselfish comment deeply moving and also realised that we were both in shock. For the next two hours the phone rang incessantly. I was on autopilot and as soon as I would replace the receiver it would ring again, it was impossible even to respond to the dozens of messages that had accumulated on the answer machine. I had become so engrossed in the unfolding saga that I had completely forgotten that there was a film camera stuck in my face. My doctor had recently prescribed beta-blockers for high blood pressure and both Helen and I must have consumed about a week's supply in a matter of hours. It soon became apparent that the remains discovered were those of Eamon Molloy from North Belfast. This was the lad we had never heard of that was on the IRA list. As the day dragged in at a hectic pace, every news bulletin carried the story and I had become physically ill with attending to the relentless pressure of the Press.

The chosen location for the return of Molloy's body was Faughart Cemetery, just north of Dundalk. Fr Alex and another cleric had walked into Dundalk Garda Station and announced the whereabouts of Molloy's remains. The body was then retrieved in a recently purchased coffin in a corner of the Cemetery.

The time of the surrender of the remains was two hours too early to qualify for the amnesty, which did not come into effect until 9 a.m. Either this fact evaded the IRA, or they weren't too bothered. The RUC announced that they were on standby and I began to receive calls from senior Garda officers. They were adamant that all the nine victims' bodies were to be located in the Republic. We had not been prepared for this and immediately began questioning how the IRA could have moved the bodies from their shallow graves in the North through roadblocks etc. to the South. Up to that point we honestly believed that all the remains would be discovered in coffins at locations such as the first. As that horrible night progressed, we heard more and more speculation about how and where we would find the victims.

The next morning, 29 May 1999, was to be every bit as hectic as the previous day, if not more so. The Gardaí once again called us to say they were investigating sites which had been pinpointed by the intermediaries, although they refused to say which individual was supposed to be interred on which site. The placenames that the media flashed up meant nothing to us, Bragan and Colgagh in Co. Monaghan, Oristown Bog and Coghalstown Co. Meath, Ballynultagh in Co. Wicklow and Templetown in Co. Louth.

An Agonising Wait

On hearing the names, Helen immediately wanted to set off for Templetown. It seems that she instinctively knew that this was where her mother was reputedly buried. The Gardaí had promised that as soon as they knew for sure who was where, they would call straight away. I therefore tried to get Helen to stay put for a little while longer.

In the meantime, she called her brother Mickey who soon arrived to join the ever-growing crowd who fell silent every time I answered a phone call. Finally we decided to grab what we could, and head for Co. Louth, as we could not bear to sit at home any longer. With the film crew on board, in front and behind we began our journey into the unknown. The cavalcade came to a screeching halt every time my mobile phone rang and this manoeuvre was repeated every couple of miles. We had just crossed into the Irish Republic when I finally received the call; as Helen had guessed, Templetown was indeed the site that they were going to excavate for Jean's remains.

I found it extremely difficult to adjust my ears to the unfamiliar accent of the Chief Superintendent, Michael Finnegan and I just about deciphered his accent to get the vaguest of directions.

Selfishly I began to try and question my feelings at the time; was it joy or trepidation? I really had no idea what to think or feel, although I did possess a certain amount of pride in the knowledge that I was keeping the promise I had made all those years ago, when I confidently swore that one day I would find Helen's mother for her.

The road from Carlingford to Templetown was nothing short of a labyrinth and our conversation was taken up trying to figure out how anyone could have found the place in the first instance. On arrival at Templetown Beach I was shocked by its limitless charm; how could somewhere so serene be hidden from the general public?

The welcomes and introductions were confusing and ultimately lost on me as I tried to distinguish between the various alien brogues. Yet the humanity of these strangers was immediate, the warmth and sympathy of these officers camouflaged their ranks as senior officers.

We found ourselves in a large carpark about 100 m by 30 m, which straight away looked outlandish in the context of such a secret place. The area to be excavated was hidden by blue polythene-covered screens. Overall's hid the personalities of the enthusiastic Gardaí who were already using a scanning machine to seek out voids in the tarmacadam. Helen took one look at the paraphernalia and the awful reason for our visit hit home; she was forced to hide her eyes from everyone by staring out to sea. She had sworn many times that the Provisionals would never have the pleasure of watching her cry. It was a heartbreaking moment and I must confess I was glad when her brother offered her a previously unknown moment of compassion.

My fascination with forensic science allowed me to 'stand outside' the proceedings, as I forced myself to concentrate on the technical aspect of things. How deep could the scanner penetrate? Was the information given written down? Could we be sure that the parking bay we were about to excavate was the right one? For an hour or so I pestered the poor Gardaí with my childish questions until the pneumatic drills drowned me out. For the remainder of the day we simply watched as wheelbarrow after wheelbarrow of tar, pebble and sand was taken to one side for raking and sifting by other members of the search team. I really had a deep feeling of sympathy for these people whose normal days would have been spent searching for arms and explosives. The way they carried on without the usual banter you would expect to accompany a group working together was a mark of respect for Helen and her family. Their dignity impressed me a great deal. We were used to a hard-line type of policing and had really never encountered compassion in a uniform before.

Local people had begun to turn up and I feared they were there for some ghoulish reason. I was very quickly proved wrong as they exuded a warmth that I hadn't detected in the human kind for quite some time. Their only intrusions were to enquire if we needed anything to eat or drink. Surely the killers of Jean McConville could not possibly have been born of this community. We were soon informed of the abhorrence that the people of the Cooley peninsula had for the Provisional IRA. One of their own people, Tom Oliver, a small farmer, had been murdered in recent years by the 'Revolutionaries'; his 'crime', it appeared, was to report a suspicious object on his land to the Gardaí. His body was discovered near to the border having been beaten, bound and shot. The people of Cooley made it abundantly clear that our grief was also theirs and they were at our service, no matter what was required. We were truly very deeply touched.

As the day wore on, the number of Press people and photographers became impossible to count and, it must be said, their empathy was equal to that of the locals. Besides, all but a very few were already known to Helen and I and had run stories on us for many years now. Other members of the McConville family were sporadically appearing on the beach. My suspicions that I was aggrieving them by agreeing to requests for television interviews were proved correct when some reporters were not so politely told to back off. This was nothing short of ridiculous as without the Press the world would never have heard of their mother. The situation became untenable and it was decided to call another family meeting, this time in McKevitts Hotel in Carlingford. Amazingly, I too was asked to attend, although I rather wished I hadn't been.

It was the usual farce, with each trying to shout the other down, but they did all manage to have an individual say. The agenda that had been discussed just a couple of weeks back was raised again, namely the proposed funeral arrangements. Once again, they unanimously agreed that things should be done as Helen suggested initially. They also agreed to uphold the decision taken and promised not to renege after leaving the room. They asked that I continue to speak on their behalf, as I had been doing so publicly for six years and privately for many, many more. Besides, I had been the spokesperson for *Families of the Disappeared* since its inception and would continue in this role as long as I was needed.

Upon returning to the beach, it soon became clear that the 'agreement' was already crumbling, as we knew it would. We blamed the documentary team for a lot of this as they insisted on heading every way but the right way about making the programme. Robert, now the eldest of the family, began to do the big brother bit and tried to dismiss both Helen and I to the sidelines. His anger would intensify when reporters would request an interview with myself or Helen and it soon deteriorated into a scene where verbal abuse was being hurled in front of news teams. They were, of course, entitled to speak about their mother and the ensuing trauma. I just couldn't understand why they had asked me to speak on their behalf if they were going to push me aside when the time came and why, when we needed it most, they hadn't offered any support during our campaign. My main concern was for Helen and I returned to be with her.

Meanwhile, the excavation had reached over a vast area of the carpark, the original pinpointed location was now lost in the tonnes of sand that had been sifted and cleared away. Almost daily, we would have our hopes raised as parts of bone or even full skeletons would be discovered. They invariably turned out to be the remains of animals, both domestic and feral, that had been buried over the years.

The strain on Helen was beginning to tell, we had stayed in just about every guest house in the Carlingford area and kept moving on as we couldn't get the owners to accept payment. This was coming up to the peak holiday period and it just wasn't fair to impose on the good nature of these people. Eventually, a local man very generously gave us the use of his mobile home, which was just a short distance from the beach. How we can ever think of reimbursing Sandy for his hospitality I will never know. Now we could bring our children down to stay with us, which saved us worrying about them being at home alone.

One might feel that spending a day by the sea would be somewhat relaxing, but these days were anything but, both Helen and I walked around in a stupor, totally fatigued. Sleepless nights were followed by half-sleeping days, the sheer monotony of concentrating on the excavation was exhausting in itself. The first two days of the search, the Gardaí dug by hand and we soon realised that we weren't going to progress very quickly.

Our initial hopes of retrieving her body within the forty-eight hours that had been suggested, were now looking extremely faint. I suspected that the team wanted to bring in machinery to speed up the excavation, but didn't say so for fear of upsetting us. Jean McConville was dead, there was no doubt about that, and no more damage could be done to her, so we gave our permission to bring in the machinery. Our only real fear was of destroying evidence if her remains were disturbed by the excavators. We needn't have worried, the operators showed a skill second to none and were able to skim off just a couple of inches at a time.

The word coming from the other search sites was pretty grim. Unlike Templetown, which was relatively easy digging as it was only sand, the other areas pinpointed were bogland and the Gardaí were having serious problems with waterlogging.

One of my most poignant memories of this time was of a rosary being said at the beach. Fr McGrain, the local parish priest, relayed the wish of his congregation to hold a service at eight o'clock. This was actually inconvenient as we had decided to drive home that evening, but we delayed our travel plans as we didn't want to appear ungrateful. I waited with the rest of the family for the locals to appear but at five past eight a sense of despair was setting in. By ten past, the priest and half a dozen parishioners had appeared. Did the search for Jean mean so little? Were people so apathetic? I honestly thought of getting into the car at this point. Suddenly, the sea mist that had shrouded the area for the previous hour began to lift and we were elated to see dozens of people walking towards us from the strand and over the sand dunes. I despised myself instantly for having doubted these lovely people, some of whom had walked miles just to show respect and offer their prayers.

When the prayer's finished, men, women and children stood in line to shake our hands and offer their hope that the search would be successful. One lady cried openly as she told me how sorry she was for having played here as a child. This statement I found deeply disturbing, how could these fine people feel that they had to apologise for the barbarity of a few psychopaths?

We soon learned that these caring people had organised a collection and the monies raised were left in McKevitts Hotel to ensure that we would have a daily meal to sustain us for the long agonising days to come. The sheer benevolence of the

Cooley folk never ceased to amaze us. Cards of sympathy and well-wishing letters arrived daily and the postman had even begun delivering to the portacabin that had been supplied by the Gardaí to protect us from the elements.

In the Hotel, there was a wall hanging which showed extracts from the writings of Irish authors. The refrain of Yeats's poem struck a chord with us and seemed to sum up how we were feeling at the time.

> *Come away, O human child!*
> *To the waters and the wild*
> *With a faery hand in hand.*
> *For the world's more full of weeping than you*
> *can understand*

From The Stolen Child *by W. B. Yeats*

Every morning around 6.30, I went for a walk on the beach, always hoping to discover that something had shifted overnight which would present a clue to the whereabouts of Jean's remains. This early morning saunter was the only time that I had a break from the Press and it also allowed Helen to attempt much needed sleep. The scenery was breathtaking and had it not been for the horror that had occurred here, I could easily have described it as blissful.

The information given by the Provisionals was that the body had been buried about five feet under a pinpointed parking bay. This had proven false as by now we had excavated it and practically all of the remainder of the parking lot. I implored the intermediaries to go back to the IRA and demand that they return to the beach to more accurately mark the spot. The message was conveyed and we were told they were mystified as to why we had not uncovered the body. They did, however, say that the burial party had driven as far as the old laneway would allow. This was all before the carpark had been constructed in 1987. They had then walked over a rivulet, or spring, and buried the body in an area devoid of vegetation which resembled a sand trap on a golf course. Once again, people who had lived at the beach in the early seventies were asked to attempt to pinpoint where the laneway had terminated. We also scrutinised old snapshots from thirty years ago that had been provided by holidaymakers of the time.

Things were not going as we had hoped and I once again called upon those individuals within the Provos who had, up to now, been sympathetic and helpful. They all agreed that we were not being intentionally misled. Sinn Féin were, at this time, deeply engrossed in the European elections and hoping that their candidate, Mitchell McLaughlin, would be successful. They were hardly going to purposely mislead us, I was told, as it would certainly not have helped them win over voters. As luck would have it, the search team discovered remnants of the old road, the ruts were easily recognised and it wasn't too difficult to ascertain were it had concluded. Just past it there was a small spring and we really felt we were close to finding the body. For the next few days we refused to take our eyes off the digging, even for a second, but alas we had no success.

The latest spurt of fruitless activity around the laneway had demoralised the Gardaí as well as ourselves, and as much as they tried to put a brave face on things, we could sense that they felt it was like looking for a pebble on a beach. Without further, more accurate details I felt that poor Jean would forever evade us despite our efforts.

The digging had begun some four weeks previously and it really did feel like we were 'going nowhere fast'. To pass the time, Helen talked me into building a shrine from beach rocks. This hurriedly erected piece of Christian art suddenly became a focus for the Press and I deeply regretted not putting more effort into it. People also started to adorn it with prayers and religious relics and I feared it was going to be there for eternity.

Instead of becoming an object of solace, the shrine was to bring us even more grief when one of the Sunday papers ran an article accompanied by a photo of Helen and I and our children at the site. Mickey, who I thought possessed a bit of sense, demanded to know why there was a picture of us and not any of the others. I remember thinking how infantile such a comment sounded.

I told him to take it up with the paper's editor. I also pointed out that perhaps they had wanted a picture of the McKendry family, since it was this family that had begun the campaign to find the truth about all of 'the disappeared'. This particular episode ended with one of the younger brothers throwing a punch at Helen; thankfully the Gardaí were close by on their tea break. This was getting seriously out of control and it was obvious that someone (most likely me) was going to get hurt.

Every politician and dignitary who had visited the site had lauded praise on us for the way we had conducted affairs since we first went public back in 1994. The Press and Clergy were the same. It saddened me that the brothers didn't conduct themselves well. Of course, everyone was stressed out, what with the heat and the sheer anxiety of the wait, but their behaviour was not helping anyone. I found it hard to understand. At first I wondered if it was a manifestation of guilt they may have had at never lifting a finger to find their mother. I began to suspect that an announcement by the Northern Ireland Memorial Fund, that it would be prepared to assist with funeral expenses to the tune of four thousand pounds if a body was recovered, had something to do with it. Helen had already stated that she would not accept the money when the time came. She believed the offer to be sincere and well intended, but as we had come this far without financial assistance, we would lay Jean to rest ourselves. Her siblings could kill each other over the payment if they wished.

The anger subsided somewhat with the news that the Victims Commission had arranged a meeting for 29 June 1999 at the Ballymascanlon Hotel in Dundalk. We all suspected that the purpose of the meeting was to inform the families of the closure of the digs. We waited with bated breath while the Gardaí showed aerial footage of the excavations and discussed the more technical data as well as problems they had encountered. The excavations were now into their fourth agonising week and everyone, including myself, was disillusioned and tired. They explained to us that what little information they received had been explored exhaustively. We all knew that when we would return from the lunch that was provided we would be told the digs were terminated. Needless to say, few of us had any appetite for food. My mobile rang and, excusing myself from the table, I went for a short stroll as I suspected it was a reporter and didn't wish to speak to him in front of the families.

True enough, it was a reporter, but instead of asking me for a story he was giving me wonderful news: 'We have just discovered human remains in the bog at Colgagh, it seems like feet bones and footwear.' I was so elated I never even caught the name of the caller, only that he was from the Press Association.

This was the location where my childhood buddies Bugsy and Bru were allegedly buried. Bugsy's mother, Mary McClory, was present at the meeting with some of her family and I raced to tell them the news. The Commissioners must have received a call too as the McClorys had already been summoned. When I related the news to the remaining families, it was received with a mixed response; some were clearly angry that I should have known before the family concerned, but in the main everyone was too overjoyed at the news for squabbling. This signified to us that the IRA had indeed given, albeit vaguely, the correct areas for the discovery of our loved-ones' remains.

Whatever the Commission had intended telling us after lunch, was rapidly put on hold, as none of us could wait another minute to return to the beach. We discovered the search teams in an euphoric mood, like ourselves, they no longer felt they would be digging in vain.

It soon filtered through that the State Pathologist, Dr Harbison, on his arrival at Colgagh, discovered that there were two bodies, one lying on top of the other in the peaty grave. It would be months before positive identifications would be made, but we all knew in our hearts that John McClory and Brian McKinney's remains had been found. The families could now grieve properly and the parents could bury their sons with the Christian dignity that everyone deserved.

Sadly, the optimism that had prevailed since the two lads had been found began to dwindle as the hours went by. We felt that we would be recalled to the Ballymascanlon for the inevitable news any day now. All the most likely parts on the beach had been tried and, apart from a narrow strip that ran parallel to the sand dunes, we believed we had done all that was humanly possible.

By 17 July, the forty-ninth day of the search, we had excavated, sifted and searched some 200,000 metric tonnes of sand; an area about the size of two Olympic-sized swimming pools. The searchers sometimes reached depths of four metres. If we were going to discover the body, I suspected it would be by accident rather than by design. That day we were informed of the expected meeting with Wilson and Bloomfield, the Commissioners. I think all who attended expected that some of the digs would be stopped. None of us imagined the suspension of the searches would be across the board, and so immediate.

We were gutted. I protested that not all the area designated had been explored. Chief-superintendent Michael Finnegan, like his men around him, stared blankly at the ground, they were every bit as disappointed as we were and weren't slow to tell us so. On hearing of my protest over the as yet unexplored area by the dunes, Finnegan ordered that his team bring the machines from the top of the beach and search where I had indicated. This was an extremely risky thing for him to do; he had, after all, been ordered to suspend immediately. This man's spirit and compassion touched us deeply, he was prepared to face disciplinary action in order to appease me.

Until 7.30 p.m. that evening I stood in the trench with the searchers, engrossed now even more than I had previously been, as I knew we were racing against the clock. I have never felt such sadness as I did that evening when the Gardaí, who by now had become like family to us, reluctantly stored up their tools and supplies. Try as they might, they couldn't say sorry or goodbye because, like ourselves, they were overcome with emotion. All we could manage were warm handshakes, the lumps in our throats too painful for words. In previous weeks, on Saturday evenings, we had accompanied the Gardaí to *Lily Finnegans*, a local pub where we discussed everything from the week's excavation to how their children were doing at school or their preference for the All-Ireland Final. They really were a decent bunch and it was a pleasure to have a couple of Guinnesses with them. Even to this day, at every given opportunity Helen and I make *'Lily's'* our first port of call, but that particular Saturday, no one was in any mood for socialising.

Incidentally, Mitchell McLaughlin's narrow failure in his bid for a seat in Europe was due directly, I believe, to the outrage generated by the horrific scenes at the search sites.

LAYING TO REST

Our feelings of deep despair and failure meant there was little conversation on our journey home. This would be the time for re-charging our batteries, or so we thought.

Eamon Molloy's body was released on the Monday and the weeks of rest and meditation we so badly needed were put on hold. Even now, we felt in a predicament; the Molloys, we had been informed, were a staunchly Republican family and we began to doubt whether our presence at the funeral would be appreciated. Later that day we would receive a call from Fr Pat McCafferty which put an end to our apprehensions. The Molloy family had expressed to him their hope that we would attend the funeral. They were, in fact, rather insistent.

It was now almost eight weeks since his body had been taken for post-mortem. The high incidence of young males who had been secretly buried, meant that the techniques applied had to be particularly thorough for a positive identification. I have to admit, it felt rather strange putting on my suit with accompanying black tie to pay my respects to someone whom I had never known, in fact never even heard of until the IRA admitted to killing him.

At the time his body was discovered, Gerry Adams was quoted in *The Independent* as saying: '[Mr Molloy] was an informer and that is something which is reviled in all aspects of society on this island.'

Apparently not everyone agreed, a huge crowd thronged the Church and surrounding streets as the cortège arrived for his requiem mass. Fr Pat McCafferty, now based in the parish, conducted the service without condemning the IRA as I had expected. His dignified alternative was both thought-provoking and praiseworthy. He went to great lengths to explain the pain that those left behind must be enduring. At Belfast City Cemetery we were asked if we would join the immediate family at the graveside. This was a break from tradition, as only the closest relatives would normally be accorded such a privilege. We were deeply touched by this suggestion and of course gratefully complied. Their sorrow was ours and we felt the need to commiserate with them.

Sadly, Eamon's mother, Susie, was so overcome with emotion and stress that she had to be taken home early and we never had the chance to say all the things we wanted on this sombre occasion. We received many thanks for our endeavours, though we made it clear that we only worked to make life more tolerable for the families and didn't need to be applauded for illustrating basic humanity.

The meeting that the Commission had promised would occur in four weeks never materialised. At first we were told it was due to holiday arrangements. I thought 'lucky them', I couldn't remember our last vacation. Then we were informed that the Commission had moved office. These might well have been genuine reasons, but they seemed hollow considering claims that the Commission was sympathetic and understanding of the families' needs. The promised updates just didn't happen and we were left to wonder whether the excavations would ever be re-opened. When I called the other families, I found them every bit as upset as we were at the complete lack of communication. Desperate to end this discourteous treatment, I asked the Press to highlight what was happening. When they did, I wasn't the Commission's favourite person, but at least we began to receive the occasional phone call. Although they told us very little, we were assured that something was being done on our behalf and that communication with the Provos was ongoing.

I have always maintained that the issue of 'the disappeared' was politicised in that it was raised or dropped to suit what was going on in the politics of Ireland. Both the British and Irish Governments wanted to bring the IRA to the political fore and I believe we were pushed aside to accommodate the smooth running of affairs. The Unionists had enough of a battering stick with the decommissioning issue without adding 'the disappeared' to their agenda.

Even the intermediaries seemed determined to silence things. Alex often asked that I stop attacking the Republican Movement as things were being done and badgering them only complicated matters. I disagreed, and reiterated my determination not to be censored, whether intentionally or not.

The Seamus Ruddy case also led me to believe that the two Governments were somehow playing funny politics. The IRSP had, for quite some time, been hounding the Commission about its lack of action in retrieving Ruddy's body. They had claimed to have visited what was once an arms dump in a forest at Bois de Boulogne near Rouen in France. They marked Ordnance Survey maps and even took video pictures to ensure there would be no error and that his body could be retrieved quickly. The Commission claims to this day that the problem lies with French bureaucracy, which is legendary. The last dig for Ruddy's body was carried out on 30 May 2000 and lasted for a paltry ten hours. I would be pretty hard to convince that the Ruddy case wasn't seen as secondary to the others, who were IRA victims and thereby more likely to have an effect on the Peace Process.

The Gardaí and the Commission had by now compiled a series of quite detailed questions. These included things that we had demanded to know at the time of the searches, such as: Was the body wrapped in a carpet? How deep was she interred? Were the killers/burial party familiar with the area? It would take time for the questionnaire to reach its intended subjects and perhaps even longer to get a reply.

This was, for Helen at least, the most difficult period of the whole campaign. The days were crawling in and we became prisoners once again, afraid to pop out in case we would miss the all-important phone call that might provide the answers we so desperately needed.

At these times, my mind oftened wandered to the far away fields of Australia and Holland where I might have lived without the hostility I was now forced to endure.

It was at this time that we heard of the demise of Maureen Kearney. This lady, although a staunch Republican, had, back in 1974, taken Helen into her home when she had nowhere else to go. Maureen, her husband Tommy and their family had been friends to both of us for many years now. Maureen had recently turned her back on the 'Revolutionaries' after her son Andrew had been murdered in a particularly cowardly and brutal attack. Andrew had quarrelled with a well-known North Belfast Provo who, in an act of revenge, ordered that Andrew be shot and the escalator to his high-rise apartment be jammed so that medical attention could not be administered. By the time it was, it was too late.

When she visited us during our ordeal at Templetown Beach, it was patently obvious that she had succumbed to the pressures of campaigning for justice for Andrew. She was a mere shadow of her former self. I begged her for the sake of her remaining family and, indeed, her own health, to give up her just but debilitating crusade. Maureen made it clear that her only thoughts were for Helen and the others who were searching for their loved ones. I was so worried by her appearance that I offered her my jacket, but being the fighter she was she declined and, instead asked us to forgive her for believing the IRA version of Jean's disappearance back in

1972. Poor Maureen would leave this life on 31 August 1999 with what is commonly known as a broken heart. The next day the remains of both Brian McKinney and John McClory were returned to their families.

Their bodies had been discovered at Colgagh, Co. Monaghan on 29 June. Both the lads were found to have been weighed down with rocks and then earthed over. McKinney's hands had been bound and they had both been shot in the head. They had lain at the site since their executions, a far cry from the supposed burial site at Glen Colin in Andersonstown, once again illustrating the Provos' expertise at misinforming.

It was going to be a busy week for funerals. In Northern Ireland you might well find that the most worn part of your wardrobe is your mourning suit with accompanying black tie.

Maureen had a wonderful, dignified send off. There were representatives from many anti-terror and human rights groups. They were a very well-known family and the huge crowd of mourners endorsed this. We were caught very much unawares when her daughters, Eleanor, Mary and Lisa asked if Helen would assist them in the carrying of their mother's remains to the Church. As much as she felt honoured to be asked to participate, she reluctantly declined. Although Helen and Maureen had known each other for a long time, Helen felt that some might think she was using the funeral to further the case of 'the disappeared'. Thankfully they understood. The presence of the McClorys and McKinneys was nice to see as I'm sure they had more than enough going on with the preparations for the burials of their own sons.

At the funeral of John 'Bugsy' McClory the next day I would once again meet men who had chummed around with us when we were lads. Quite a few of these had been through the ranks of the Provos, but there was absolutely no animosity towards us, quite the opposite in fact. When one individual with a pretty chequered past came over to shake my hand and thank me for my efforts in retrieving Bugsy's body, I felt deeply moved.

Shortly after the interment, the 'brothers grim' told Fr Alex that they had no faith in either him or the Commission and they had new information which placed Jean McConville's remains half a mile away from Templetown, in the foundations of the M1 at Westlink, and they had a map to prove it!

The same faces from my youth were to be seen the following day when Bru McKinney was laid to rest, also in Milltown Cemetery. The relief, if not happiness, on the faces of the two boys' mothers was clear to be seen; they had laid their sons to rest in proper graves in a Christian manner. Their struggle for peace of mind was over and I felt I had at last done something positive in my life. However, we had only won a couple of battles; the war was yet to be completed.

With no communication worthwhile with the Commission, it was left to Alex to carry titbits of information back to us. He, like ourselves, dismissed the brothers' M1 theory as he knew 'for certain' that the IRA had not lied when they gave the locations of 'the disappeared'. Quite apart from anything else, the motorway link wasn't conceived, never mind constructed, until many years after their mother's demise. Even though they were aware of the many false trails we had been sent on over the years, they were still prepared to listen to idle rumour. I wondered why they couldn't just join forces and help us demand the truth via a concerted effort. I did know that I couldn't take much more of this pulling and pushing.

As if the discord wasn't bad enough, Helen knew that this was only the beginning. In the event of Jean's body being found, the fireworks would really begin; they had made it clear to Helen that they would deprive her of the burial right. If only she could believe that the body was at Templetown, then she could erect a memorial and get on with her life.

Once again, we returned to the awful sitting about. It was soul destroying, a cancerous silence, and I began to worry now about the long-term effect it was having on Helen. She had been diagnosed as suffering from ME a couple of years previously and only a fool wouldn't see it as a direct result of the strain of the search. I often thought of how quickly death had visited upon poor Maureen Kearney. We regularly talked about what the future might bring. If we retrieved the body, we knew there would be family arguments to determine who had the right to arrange the funeral. On the other hand, if we were unsuccessful, would Helen be able to say 'we tried' and live with that?

It was late Autumn now and conversation with Alex was upbeat as he had returned to the sites with the IRA and he was convinced of their sincerity in wishing to find the remains. It appeared they had responded quite well to the questionnaire and I looked forward to seeing what light they had shed on the mystery. It would be November, however, before I would see the response.

Alex asked Helen if she wished to leave the room, as some of the details might upset her. 'No', she replied, 'I have to hear this.' He could hardly contain himself as he began to read through the questionnaire. He had worked damn hard to get this response and was relishing his moment. My earlier suspicions that this man could not be trusted to remain impartial had gone. He was adamant that the Provisionals knew it was an issue that they had created and that they must clear up. Granted, Jean's funeral would be a major embarrassment to them, given that I had made it patently clear that I wanted news crews from all over the globe to be there. The alternative was to mislead us about the burial site, but this could work against them if her body were found accidentally someplace else. We had made them look fool enough, without them taking the chance of incurring the wrath of world leaders for leading us 'up the garden path'.

Part of me expected the answers to be half-baked and was very surprised to read their responses to the well-thought-out questions.

Q. Can you say with clarity that Jean McConville is interred on Templetown beach and not someplace else?

A. It has been suggested, that our members might have mistaken Templetown for the nearby Shelling Hill, this is not even a possibility, they drove the road from Greenore, the remains are where indicated.

Q. Did the burial party have good, middling or poor local knowledge?

A. Very good local knowledge.

Q. Was the burial party from the locality?

A. Irrelevant.

Q. Did the burial party return to the site soon after the burial?

A. Yes.

Q. Have the burial party returned to the site in recent times?

A. Yes.

Q. At what time of the day did the burial take place?

A. It was at twilight.

Q. Can you describe the terrain, immediately surrounding the grave?

A. It was devoid of vegetation, quite similar in appearance to a sand bunker on a golf course.

Q. Was the body wrapped in anything, i.e. carpet, plastic or sacking?

A. No.

Q. Was the body clothed?

A. Yes.

Q. Was there anything in the line of jewellery or metal buckles?

A. No.

Q. How deep was it buried?

A. Two to three feet.

Q. Can you say in what direction the body was placed, in regards to the shoreline?

A. The body was buried with the feet towards the sea, i.e. in a North-South direction.

Q. How far up the beach did they actually travel?

A. To the end of the old track/laneway only.

Q. How deep was the body buried and in what material?

A. About two and a half feet in pure sand.

Q. The burial party consisted of how many?

A. Not applicable.

Q. Have all the individuals involved in the affair been spoken to?

A. Most definitely yes. Down to the last man, Everyone was spoken to and all responded honestly.

I have simplified some of the answers as they were quite long-winded and in a multiple-choice type format. Their responses were more detailed than they needed to be and they chose to ignore only a few questions. This was nothing short of astonishing when one considers that this exercise was repeated for the other victims too. Were they really ashamed of what their comrades of the earlier days had done? Or was this all just an exercise to pretend they had tried? I couldn't be sure.

Although I wanted to believe them, it was difficult considering how many times I had listened to their fabrications in the past.

Helen would sleep little over the next week as she played the horrific saga over and over again in her mind. She expressed delight at the knowledge that her mother's body had been clothed, only to start doubting again an hour later. She had read enough about the brutality shown to women in wars all around the globe and figured the Provos would be capable of anything that went on in places like the Balkans or East Timor. She believed that women and children were exempt from the ravages of men's wars; to a degree, men were expected to suffer or even die in their haste for power and control.

Her mother had now joined the list of young Irish women who had been horrifically killed in the name of revolution over the past thirty years. Anne Ogilvy was beaten to death whilst her little daughter listened outside the door to her mother's screams in what became known as the 'Romper Room' killing. Anne Marie Smith, the young, single mother-of-two lured to the Ravenhill Road with talk of a party, was savagely beaten and had her throat cut. She was dumped on waste ground at Ballarat Street. Her 'crime' was being a Catholic.

Equally barbaric was the horrific murder of Margaret Wright, tortured by the Red Hand Commando, a UVF splinter group, in a shebeen. Her twisted remains were unceremoniously dumped in a wheelie bin. Her 'crime' was to be mistaken for a Catholic. The three-man gang that murdered Margaret Perry and secretly buried her body in Co. Sligo were, after confessing, killed by the IRA. In more recent times, we saw the 'execution' of mother-of-three Caroline Mulholland from Belfast, for allegedly passing on information to the security forces.

A FAMILY DIVIDED

Christmas is always a very special time in Helen's calendar, not for the religious connotation, but because it is a time of year that had, in the past, brought nothing but sadness; her father's sickness and death and then her mother's disappearance. Every year she infuriated me by going to unbelievable lengths to overdo the festivities and it is only in recent years that I discovered that she wanted to block out the past horrors and make sure our own family felt happy and secure. In 1999, however, Christmas was different, something was missing, and even our children sensed it.

We were to enter the new millennium full of hope, our little granddaughter Tiegan had been born to our eldest daughter Kellyanne on 23 May 1998, the same day the Parties in the North and, indeed, the whole of Ireland signed the Good Friday Agreement. I remember joking that she would be walking by the time the Agreement Parties actually agreed on anything, although as time went on I began to think it might not happen until Tiegan's own grandchildren were walking.

Still stuck in the decommissioning quagmire, it didn't seem like any of the Parties wanted to allow her a peaceful future. The years of conflict had provided some with very lucrative incomes and they weren't going to relinquish their spoils easily.

Finally, we received a call from the Commission and on 12 February we found ourselves back in the Ballymascanlon Hotel. They would begin by apologising for the 'poor' communication, without offering any reason for it. They had scrutinised the questionnaires and were happy to say that the digs would re-open soon. Perimeters had been drawn and they indicated that the searches would be concluded in about three weeks. They also indicated that they had acquired a specific piece of information regarding one of the sites, though they refused to elaborate.

We would hear from them in two weeks, both by phone and letter, to clarify the actual resumption date, or so we were told. We were surprised not to see Helen's brothers at the meeting, though we were later accused of keeping information of the meeting from them, which was quite extraordinary really, as they had assured us that they had their own line of communication with the Commission. Anyway, weren't these the guys who had expressed no faith in that body?

The only visit we had was when a tabloid carried a story about this book being written. They demanded to know why I had not asked their advice on the contents. To begin with, Helen is the only one of the family to have raised the issue of her mother's disappearance and her powers of recall are second to none, in fact, I have never known anyone with such a fantastic and accurate memory. The book is, in part, an insight into the sad short life of Jean McConville and who better to tell it than the daughter who was undoubtedly closest to her. Also, it was Helen and I that had campaigned for the truth about those that had disappeared in Northern Ireland so why would I seek comment from individuals who had not supported our campaign.

There were phone calls to our home in the middle of the night promising all sorts of unpleasantness. For some five years now, I had promised Helen that I would give her mother a voice, a voice that had been denied her by the IRA back in 1972 and with Helen's blessing and essential input it is what I have done.

Knowing the resumption of the digs was imminent, I hastily painted the piece of marble I had acquired some time back. It read:

> In memory of our beloved Mother Jean McConville, taken from us by the IRA on 7 December 1972, and believed buried on this beach.

It was a small gesture, but something that meant a lot to Helen and I could see the pride on her face as we concreted it to the shrine on the beach. By the first week in March, we had the written confirmation that we had been waiting for; the excavations were to resume at all the original sites, though they didn't say when. They had digested the contents of the questionnaires and felt it was worth having another attempt. They did, however, advise all the families against building up their hopes.

Alex was now almost a daily caller and felt sure that when the weather improved and the days lengthened we would return to Templetown for 'a period of around forty-eight hours'.

On 2 May, a Tuesday, we set off yet again in search of Jean's remains, though this time we lacked the enthusiasm that prevailed at the first search. We were accompanied by a good friend, Michael Mann; one of those unselfish individuals who had, over the years, trodden the streets with us in the demand for truth.

We knew that we would be likely to face further animosity from the 'brothers grim' as they had released statements to the Press in the previous week claiming they had absolutely no confidence in the Commission. This was followed by a lengthy communication to the *Irish News* and *Sunday Life* which claimed that I had been axed as their spokesman. I laughed at it all, although Helen was quite incensed. She was quick to tell journalists that it was okay for me to be the brothers' spokesman when it meant putting someone's life on the line, but now, with all the publicity and therefore reduction in threat, they wanted me out of the way.

They should have known by now that I don't succumb to intimidation and the threatening calls in the middle of the night only made me more determined than ever to stand by my wife. The phone calls of support from some of the other suffering families, beseeching me to stay on track and lauding praise for what had already been achieved, also encouraged me to continue.

The Press were waiting as we drove onto the strand and straight away it was obvious that, like myself, they were not optimistic. They were only there to appease their editors. I declined the offer to speak to them and explained that I did not want to give the brothers an opportunity to further humiliate the family and Helen was quite capable of speaking for herself, on questions regarding 'the disappeared'.

The Gardaí explained which area was to be excavated; a previously unexplored three-metre strip parallel to the sand dunes. These dunes were believed to have shifted over the years and it was hoped this would explain the confusion as to where the remains lay. By lunchtime, the brothers had arrived, we were up at the far end of the beach where the digging was going on while they remained at the entrance to the beach. It was a sad sight; a family so pulled apart that they couldn't even look at one another, never mind speak to each other.

It was afternoon before there was a break in the stand-off when Agnes and Tucker came over to speak with us. The reporters standing about rallied at this movement, but to give them credit, they did not intrude and allowed us to have our conversation in private. Incensed by the actions of his brother and sister, Jim decided to enter the scene. He was quick to point out that he and his brothers (at least most of them) were very aggrieved at certain things. I walked off with him to try and get things sorted. I half expected a punch in the mouth and if I got one I wanted it to be out of sight of the cameras. He demanded that a meeting be organised to clear matters up. I totally agreed and asked who might chair the meeting as any such attempt in the past had ended in disarray. I was to learn later that day that they had approached the Gardaí to request that a senior officer act as chairperson for the meeting. When the officer discovered that the ratio was to be six of the brothers against myself, he declined, as he considered it to be nothing short of intimidation.

Number one on the agenda was this book, I agreed to return the next day to answer their questions although I knew that no matter what was sorted, it would only last for a short period. Against Helen's wishes, I was determined to have it out with them and if it meant acquiring a couple of black eyes then so be it. This was about recovering the body of their mother and not about personalities or guilt tripping. I was determined to meet them until, later that evening, I learned that they had approached the Gardaí to demand that I be forcibly removed from the beach. They were told that they would be the ones asked to leave if there was any trouble.

At this point I could see the difficult situation in which the Gardaí were being placed. They were only there to do a job, and were doing so marvellously, they didn't need to become entangled in this nonsense. I was totally sickened by the brothers' actions and vowed to never again set my foot on Templetown as long as there was one of them present. I was so disgusted by the actions that I stayed at home the following day.

Helen and Michael Mann travelled on their own to be met with the news, as told to them by Tucker (Thomas) and Agnes, that the brothers were determined to stop their mother being buried with Anne in Milltown Cemetery and had been making inquiries about having her exhumed and put with her father in

Lisburn. I can only assume that Jean's ashes were to be placed there too, but in a typical scatterbrained exercise, they had not allowed for the fact that the Lisburn grave was full to capacity and no one could be interred there for another ninety or so years. That was the reason that Anne hadn't been buried with her father in the first place.

We received a phone call that day from a lady well known to both of us, who told how she had been asked to call by the residents of Twinbrook to commend Helen for her stance and dismiss the antics of her family as hypocrisy. This message from her old neighbours was genuine and touching. Helen's response was full of hurt and her despair at her brothers' behaviour affected me deeply. She said that she had endured enough from the organisation responsible for the death of her mother, without having to take this crap from her sad siblings. 'They never once made an effort to help with the funeral expenses for Anne', she told her, 'yet they were seriously considering having the poor girl's body exhumed simply to deny me my wish to have her alongside her mum', and, it must be said, far away from the 'granny from hell' who had been the last to be laid to rest in the Lisburn Cemetery.

Was it really worth it all, the stress and strain of campaigning, to be rewarded with this? How much longer could we continue? The grapevine was informing us that the other families were at their wits' end and people's health was declining as a result. That evening, Helen requested that I assist her in the compilation of a statement to the Press that would outline our present stance.

> It is with deep sorrow that myself, wife Helen and group volunteers announce our departure from this beach today. In an effort to prevent the memory of Jean McConville and unavoidably the other poor unfortunates, collectively known as 'the disappeared' from being besmirched by the insensitive and often hostile behaviour from certain individuals.

There was no other way left to go and we went on to say how much we regretted having to leave and thanked the Gardaí and local people for their support and effort.

Even though our withdrawal was voluntary, it was incredibly difficult to stay away. Credit must be given to the Gardaí, who called us regularly to inform us of their progress.

The media coverage of the excavations suffered as a result of our leaving, which was a real pity, but to remain would have turned the whole affair into a free-for-all. We spent the time we waited constructively and talked endlessly about what had and had not been achieved to date. Was the whole search a farce? Was it the result of an agreement between the Republican Movement and the Governments simply to be seen to be trying to resolve the issue? Were they attempting to do it with as little embarrassment as possible to the culprits so that they may get on with the business of creating a peaceful assembly in the North? Helen chastised me for my pessimism and again pointed to the fact that we had already succeeded in returning three sets of remains to their families based on the information given by the Provos.

She then said something that I had been hoping to hear for years; she now knew that her mother was dead and was resigned to the fact that the body was somewhere on Templetown strand. She talked on and on about how beautiful the place was and how lucky her mum was, in a sense, to lie there. Was this as a result of being exhausted and disgusted by her siblings or did she genuinely feel this? I had to know for sure.

There would still be another two weeks or so of digging and we had to prepare for the possibility of not discovering the remains. A number of calls from the papers on 12 May 2000, alerted us to the fact that the Commission intended to curtail the searches after only two weeks. We were livid and this action only served to reinforce my view that the current digs were nothing short of a cosmetic exercise. I immediately contacted Eamon Mulligan of the Commission to voice my disgust at the flippant use of the families and to complain about receiving important information, once again, via the media. Rather than try to camouflage the action, he tried to tell me that they had progressed much quicker than had been estimated.

Thankfully, I am in the habit of keeping a journal and therefore I have a record of the content of all meetings etc. It was declared at our last meeting that the digs would resume, but for 'a period of three weeks only'. From day one we were told that money to finance these searches was not, nor never would be, a factor. If this were the case, and the Commission had budgeted to excavate for the three-week period, then why was the dig to end a week early? We felt like we were some sort of unwelcome blot on the budget; the insensitivity of these people never ceased to amaze us.

Calling around the families, I found that, like ourselves, they too felt deeply hurt at the proposed withdrawal. Resolved to face the inevitable, we were en route to the beach that Wednesday morning to thank the Gardaí for their endeavours, when Mulligan rang to tell us we had been granted an extension to Saturday 18 May, which was still five days short of the promised conclusion of Tuesday 24 May.

We were welcomed warmly but apologetically by the search teams, who still believed they were having to finish that afternoon. Many of these Gardaí expressed their disgust and disbelief at the treatment being meted out and offered to guide us around the dig to make sure we were satisfied with what had been done to date. We were satisfied, although Helen expressed a desire to have the area under and around the small shrine that we had erected the previous year explored.

We knew that without our permanent presence on the site (and of course the ensuing entourage of Press) the closure was inevitable and returning that Saturday morning was merely a formality. The Gardaí had covered a huge area of ground in the interim, no doubt wishing to be successful in the short time permitted to them. They had also carried out Helen's wish to search the area around the shrine; these guys were the salt of the earth and will remain in our thoughts forever. Apart from the obvious, the only smudge on the day was the appearance of her two youngest brothers who proceeded to hurl abuse and threats, even telling Helen to get back into the company of her 'fucking mates', the Gardaí. This was something of an irony as they were indeed mates and will remain so.

That evening, we once again collected our thoughts and pondered the next move in our lives. Helen was of the opinion that her mother was trying hard not to be found, she was mortified by the actions of her children and knew that it was better for everyone that she remain undetected on the beach. This statement might seem a bit strange to most, but knowing Helen's superstitious nature, it was a perfectly natural and sane conclusion.

This very conclusion spelt the end of our campaign and we both knew it.

Our struggle was firstly aimed at forcing the Provisional IRA to admit to the world that they had indeed murdered Jean McConville. Secondly, we demanded that they identify the burial site, this Helen believes they have done (I personally have reservations), albeit reluctantly. She concludes that the fact that the remains still lie on Templetown beach is of her mother's own choosing. After what Helen has been through, I fully understand how she came to this conclusion.

Knowing fine well that we could dig from now to doomsday and not retrieve the remains of 'the disappeared', I have nothing but admiration for Helen for allowing the other families (the majority of whom are quite elderly) the dignity of knowing we tried and allowing them to find peace in the knowledge that their sons, like her mother, are interred in some of the most beautiful locations in Ireland.

I often attempt to figure out how we could have excavated such a vast area of ground and yet failed to find her remains. Is it possible that her body was disturbed during the construction of the Templetown car park? If the information given by the Provos is correct, then she was interred at the foot of the sand dunes. This is the very place where the sewage pipes were laid alongside the tarmac. The contractors, with their super heavy machinery, would not have been looking for remains and I guess it's very possible that her body was dispersed at the site. When the search began, we were looking for a skeleton and not fine pieces of bone.

One possibility often raised is that with high Winter tides, her body could have been washed out to sea, though I would think if this had happened she would have washed up on some coastline or other.

Conclusions

On 7 December 1972, a young mother, only recently widowed, is dragged from her hysterical children at gunpoint. This thirty-seven-year-old is a totally apolitical homebird, living for her family and her home, her one 'extravagance' in life being a very rare game of bingo, when the entrance money could be spared. She had suffered terribly since her husband and soulmate died in January and meandered through bouts of chronic despair and the ensuing hospitalisation. Her only known 'crimes' against her community were her Protestant childhood and her compassion in administering a prayer in the ear of an injured British soldier.

The suggestion that she somehow colluded with the British war machine stretches credulity to the extreme. She quite simply wasn't around (she spent a large portion of her time in hospital) to have known anything and she quite simply didn't want to know anything, the war was outside, herself and her family were within. Surely any anger she might have possessed would have been concentrated on the security forces. After all, it was they who had interned her eldest son on his 17th birthday and smashed her door down on many occasions, breaking Helen's leg in one particularly zealous raid. As much as she despised violence, she was astute enough to understand that the only protection afforded to the community came via the IRA. The only real threat from paramilitaries had been from the Loyalists who had forced her to flee her home in East Belfast.

Jean McConville came to the attention of the IRA because of a wrangle over a three-piece suite. Add to this the aforementioned 'transgressions' and you have a recipe for kangaroo court justice.

What sort of information was Jean supposed to be passing? As a mother of ten young children, I contend that the only thing she was likely to posses that might be of use to the foe would be her recipes. It is nothing short of absurdity to suggest that she was in any way a danger to Provo operations in the Falls area; surely she would have to have been a member of the organisation to be acquainted with their movements. Loose talking was rife then and still is today, I have personally overheard conversations that left nothing to the imagination. Even if she was deemed guilty of this foolish practice, the punishment of the day would have been tarring and feathering, head shaving and, in the most serious of cases, exile. Poor Jean was dragged out in the presence of her screaming children and taken no doubt to a nearby 'safe house' for interrogation.

I suggest she never did get to meet the 'security team', for had she done so they would have established in a very short time that she was neither an agent or a threat to them.

Remember that Jean had first been abducted on 6 December, surely if she had been some sort of agent provocateur, military intelligence would have swiftly removed her and her family to a safe house. Is it even credible to suggest that they allowed her to return to her home knowing that her cover had been blown, even more so, would she have been foolhardy enough to return of her own free will? Remember we are talking about a young Belfast girl who left school with only a smattering of learning and not some sort of *Mata Hari*.

If she were a spy, why did she live the pitiful existence she did, hand to mouth, with ever increasing bills? Maybe I am wrong, but I was always led to believe that espionage paid handsomely.

My mind goes back to the time when I was told, on good authority, that in an attempt to frighten her, a plastic bag had been placed on Jean's head. Given her very poor state of health, it was hardly surprising to hear that she suffocated. As in the case of Nairac, a 'real' spy, where the Provos had the golden opportunity of using him for propaganda purposes, the indiscipline of the foot soldiers denied the 'security teams' the chance to interrogate him.

So what next? This gang of incompetents is left with a young woman's body, worse still they are left with the body of a woman that they are known to have abducted. This immediately rules out dumping her body by the motorway in the hope that Loyalists will be blamed. This body had to 'disappear' forever and scurrilous rumour had to be employed to ensure that no one would go looking for her.

Templetown beach, her supposed burial site, is a good sixty miles away and some of the most intense security to be found anywhere on this earth lies between there and Belfast. It was practically impossible to walk the length of a Belfast street in 1972 without being searched and checked out by the security forces. Are we really to believe that they drove from the Falls Road, with its heavy security presence, past the watchtowers of the border posts, past RUC and Army units, both overt and covert, and reached the Republic where further surveillance, in the shape of the Irish Army and the Garda Siochána, failed to detect them?

The risks involved in moving a weapon were phenomenal, never mind a body, whether dead or alive. If she were alive, there was the kidnapping and possible attempted murder rap to contend with, if she were dead, then the charge would guarantee a life sentence or two.

Or was this young woman's body taken by boat? Might this explain why the IRA claimed in its answer to the questionnaire to have driven to Templetown from Greenore, which is the area's closest harbour? The only land route from the North to the beach is via Carlingford. Remember, they also admitted that the unit involved was familiar with the locality, and therefore unlikely to take a seaward route as opposed to a land one.

I conclude that Jean McConville was 'arrested' on rumour and hearsay and subsequently killed by over-zealous imbeciles drunk on their sense of power and control or perhaps just drunk!

Although it delights me, for the sake of her sanity, to hear Helen say that she knows her mother's body lies somewhere on that beach, I believe the remains were never intended for discovery. That very brittle frame could still tell the trained eye a thing or two. Even though her body would have been desecrated with the time-honoured quicklime, I have tremendous respect for the science of forensics. Perhaps someday soon Jean's skeletal remains will present themselves for intense examination and analysis.

Will this unduly worry her killers, who have, after all, been granted a degree of immunity from prosecution? With the early release scheme for prisoners I doubt if being prosecuted for her death would really trouble the perpetrators, unless of course they are now VIPs. Who else would demand immunity? To the ordinary 'volunteer', a couple of years inside is trivial, but to someone trying to become a figurehead in a democracy, the brutal murder of Jean McConville would forever taint their political aspirations.

Sean O'Callaghan, former Chief of staff of the IRA's Southern command and serial turncoat, claimed in a CBS *60 Minutes* broadcast in America late last year that Sinn Féin leader Gerry Adams was the adjutant of the IRA's First Battalion at the time of Jean's abduction and that he most certainly knew full well the circumstances surrounding her disappearance. Now to be honest, I wouldn't give merit to anything the likes of O'Callaghan might say, this man has sold himself to the highest bidder on too many occasions, but I do, however, reckon that Mr Adams was quite senior in the IRA ranks in the early seventies.

On 21 July 2000, we loaded the children up and returned to Templetown for the first time since the search had been abandoned. It might well have been somewhere on the isle of Ibiza as it was completely thronged with half-naked bathers, the cars were parked three deep on top of the area that had been excavated so painstakingly by the Gardaí not so long ago. When your dead you're dead, but was it wrong for tourists to relax and enjoy themselves here? Life goes on after all, and Helen says her mother is here watching over the children as they joyfully scream and splash the day through. Yet the fact that the shrine we both erected in 1999 is nowhere to be seen, means there is nothing to tell these folk to be respectful in their enjoyment. In our absence at the last search, the siblings removed the little monument to facilitate the dig, now neither sibling nor shrine is to be seen.

Helen talked incessantly on the journey home about how her mum had died in vain. It was bad enough for her to find that when the list of the victims of the conflict was displayed in neon at Shaftsbury Square, Belfast, around Christmas, 'the disappeared' were never mentioned. Since the shrine had been taken down by Agnes to allow the Gardaí to excavate under it, the bathers at Templetown were denied the knowledge of the existence of Jean McConville. The little marble plaque on the shrine had quite simply read:

> In memory of our beloved Mother Jean McConville, taken from us by the IRA on 7 December 1972 and believed buried on this beach.

'It is extremely important that people know of the horror that took place there, not to dissuade holidaymakers but rather to encourage the future generations to stay far removed from the clutches of violence', the anger in Helen's voice was plain. The Provos tried for some twenty-odd years to erase the memory of her mother and by removing the shrine her family were (perhaps unintentionally), doing the same.

Meanwhile, the Commission have stated that they are quite prepared to erect memorials at the locations given so that 'the disappeared' might have a headstone of sorts and the families might find succour and the God-given right to grieve for the loved-one that was so barbarically taken from them.

The townsfolk of 'the Cooley' have, as I could have guessed, already expressed a desire to assist in erecting a fitting memorial to their adopted daughter, Jean McConville.

God bless them all.

AFTERWORD

BY HELEN MCKENDRY

In 1994, reflecting on the recent death of my eldest sister Anne, I became determined to ensure that she would be the last member of my family to go to their grave not knowing what became of my mother. My life without the truth wasn't a proper life and I decided to throw caution to the wind and tackle the killers head on. To do so, I needed support and sadly, only my husband and children were willing to stand by me, my immediate family choosing to bury their heads in the sand. If she were alive today, my mother would be only sixty-five years old. I have a great relationship with my eldest daughter Kellyanne, and I sorely miss what might have been with my mum. She was a terrific mother and would no doubt have relished being a grandmother and now a great-grandmother.

From that first visit to Templetown beach, I felt my mother was close, I enjoyed an inner peace for the first time since she had been so cruelly torn from me. Did I really want to take her from this beautiful and peaceful beach and place her in Milltown, Belfast, among the very people who had stolen her body in the first place? Anyway, it is only her remains that lie on the beach, her soul is already in residence at a finer place and someday we will be together again. Although I plan to erect a memorial to her at Templetown, I believe this book will be the proper testimony to her memory and no doubt it will be seen by more than the memorial at Templetown will be. Thanks to the warlords on all sides, I was denied even the most basic of education and therefore the ability to write this book myself. I have though, in my husband, a man of words and undoubted courage, who unselfishly fought, suffered and above all understood my insatiable need to discover the truth. My mother would no doubt be extremely proud of the son-in-law that she never did have the privilege to meet.

I hope and pray that the families of those who, like my mother, perished so needlessly can share with me in the peace of mind that I thought would never come about. Of course, I still want to know if she suffered much at the time and I would really like to know the actual date on which she died, but I also know that she wouldn't want me to throw away the short life that we are given. My only wish is that those who read this, tell those who are too young to read it, that life is far, far too precious to be wasted over a piece of land or a flag.

Song For The Disappeared

By Hugh Jordan

I close my eyes and wonder,
Imagine where you are,
Are you standing close to me,
Or have you gone afar?
The years pass on so slowly now,
But still I shed a tear,
It's the lasting bond between us,
Since the day you disappeared, since the day
you disappeared.

I still recall the little things,
Like calling out your name,
Falling out and making up,
You always got the blame,
I remember endless summer walks,
Both sweltered in the sun,
And I wish these days were here again,
When you and I were one, when you and I were
one.

Then word came through, that you had gone,
I didn't understand,
Surely all a big mistake,
None of this was planned,
An endless string of letters,
And those hours on the phone,
Until one day I realised,
You were never coming home, you were never
coming home.

This song's for John McClory,
And Brian McKinney too,
Charlie Armstrong and Gerry Evans,
The neighbour that he knew,
And also Jean McConville,
A mother once to ten,
All victims of cruel fate,
At the hands of faceless men, at the hands of
faceless men.

Love and War

Today, another blow for the cause
Some woman's husband — mother's son
Why should I pause with niggling thoughts
of who he is — was
Because, he might have just informed
on the cause.

I got an order to carry out
No hesitation, loyal to a fault
So I went about my bloody task
with head held high, no fear or
doubt, even though I knew
he had no clout.

I hid him well, beneath
the dirt and debris of our plan.
The grief and tears of those he loved
not knowing where to lay the
wreath, meant little then, but soon
we all face death.

But it's the nights — the dreams,
What if we're wrong in all these
schemes to have OUR way
against all odds, not caring who's
between, their life their death
our terror screams.

It's her again, his wife, why should I care
if she might know, just smile
and stare her out. I'm 'Jack the
Lad' in with the IN crowd, it's not
fair to have these doubts
in Love and War.

Dawn D. Quigley
25 September 1995